RELIEF | A QUARTERLY CHRISTIAN EXPRESSION

VOLUME ONE | ISSUE FOUR

RELIEF | A QUARTERLY CHRISTIAN EXPRESSION

EDITOR-IN-CHIEF
Kimberly Culbertson

TECHNICAL EDITOR
Coach Culbertson

ASSISTANT EDITOR
Heather von Doehren

EDITORIAL ASSISTANT
Margaret Krueger

FICTION EDITOR
J. Mark Bertrand

COPY EDITORS
Margaret Krueger

CREATIVE NONFICTION EDITORS
Karen Miedrich-Luo
Lisa Ohlen Harris

READERS
Mick Silva—Fiction

POETRY EDITOR
Brad Fruhauff

Relief: A Quarterly Christian Expression is published quarterly by ccPublishing, NFP, a 501(c)3 organization dedicated to advancing Christian literary writing. Mail can be sent to 60 W. Terra Cotta, Suite B, Unit 156, Crystal Lake, IL 60014-3548. Submissions are not accepted by mail.

SUBSCRIPTIONS

Subscriptions are $48 per year and can be purchased directly from the publisher by visiting http://www.reliefjournal.com. Single issues are also available.

COPYRIGHT

All works Copyright 2007 by the individual author credited. Anything not credited is Copyright 2007 by ccPublishing, NFP. No part of this publication may be reproduced, stored in a retrieval system, or transmitted by any means without prior written permission of ccPublishing, NFP.

SUBMISSIONS

Submissions are open year round via our Online Submissison System. Please visit our website at http://www.reliefjournal.com for instructions. Sorry, but we are unable to read or return submissions received by mail.

THANK YOU

We thank the following people who, by subscribing before the first issue or by donating, have financially supported *Relief*.

WE OWE EXTRAORDINARY GRATITUDE TO OUR DONORS: HEROES:

HEATHER ACKMANN
THE MASTER'S ARTIST @ HTTP://WWW.THEMASTERSARTIST.COM
ROBERT AND LAURA BAKER

AND TO THE REST OF OUR FOUNDERS, WHO HAVE HELPED US TO MAKE THIS JOURNAL A REALITY:

VASTHI ACOSTA
ADRIENNE ANDERSON
KARI L. BECKEN
JILL BERGKAMP
STEVE BOGNER
SUSAN BOYER
SUSAN H. BRITTON
SHAWN COHEN
JONATHAN D. COON
CHAD COX
JEANNE DAMOFF
DIANNA DENNIS
BEN DOLSON
STEVE ELLIOTT
CHRISTOPHER FISHER
DEEANNE GIST
DEBORAH GYAPONG
SYLVIA HARPER
APRIL HARRISON
MATTHEW HENRY
GINA HOLMES
LEANNA JOHNSON
JILL KANDEL
MICHAEL KEHOE
BILL AND PEGGIE KRUEGER
ALLISON LEAL
DAVID LONG
JEROMY MATKIN

ANDREW MEISENHEIMER
CHRISTOPHER MIKESELL
CHARMAINE MORRIS
MARGARET M. MOSELEY
SARAH NAVARRO
NANCY NORDENSON
KAREN T. NORRELL
RANDY PERKINS
SHANNA PHILIPSON
CALEB ROBERTS
SUZAN ROBERTSON
CHRISTINA ROBERTSON
LISA SAMSON
LANDON SANDY
AOTEAROA EDITORIAL SERVICES
MICHAEL SNYDER
CATHERINE STAHL
DOROTHEE SWANSON
AMBER TILSON
SHERRI TOBIAS
PHIL WADE
DAVID WEBB
CHRISTINA WEEKS
REBEKAH WILKINS-PEPITON
MARYANNE WILIMEK
MANKATO
AND THOSE WHO PREFER TO REMAIN ANONYMOUS

If you would also like to help keep the journal going, please visit our website, www.reliefjournal.com and click on Support The Cause.

TABLE OF CONTENTS

FROM THE EDITOR'S DESK KIMBERLY CULBERTSON	6
COACH'S CORNER COACH CULBERTSON	8

EDITOR'S CHOICE

SCARS CREATIVE NONFICTION BY CHRISTOPHER FISHER	10
AN ITALIAN RESTAURANT IN DOMINION POETRY BY C. A. HASSELBALCH	21
EPITHALAMIUM CREATIVE NONFICTION BY EDMUND DE CHASCA	22

FICTION

SWIMMERS INTO CLEANNESS LEAPING ALAN ACKMANN	31
A REED SHAKEN IN THE WILDERNESS DEVIN O'DONNELL	50
THE RIDER AHEAD JOSEPH LAIZURE	84
HUNDRED DOLLAR BILLS LINDA MCCULLOUGH MOORE	106
IS ANYONE ALL RIGHT? LINDA MCCULLOUGH MOORE	109

CREATIVE NONFICTION

RELINQUISHED MARGOT STARBUCK HAUSMANN	42
TORN VEIL LISA OHLEN HARRIS	58
STONING, SOUTHERN BAPTIST STYLE ELLEN HERBERT	95
.5 YEARS IN TOKYO DANNY MILLER	114

POETRY

FINDING THE RING DAVID BEDSOLE	25
MY THERAPIST SAYS I NEED TO LEARN GRACE DAVID BEDSOLE	26
PRISON WORK DAVID BEDSOLE	27
WINDOW WASHER S. R. KOVACOVIC	28
THE ATLANTIC D. S. MARTIN	30
DAPHNE'S COMPLAINT TO SRYINX SORINA HIGGINS	39
SEMELE'S EXAMPLE SORINA HIGGINS	40
WEDDING DAY SORINA HIGGINS	41
KNOWING TOO MUCH TRISTA SWING	46
PARENTS TRISTA SWING	47
THE HEALER JUDY LEE GREEN	48
THE READING KELLY BELMONTE	56
TRANSFORMATION CINDY BEEBE	67
PRELUDE NICK DUMAIS	68
I FELL IN LOVE WITH A PREACHER'S WIFE ROSS GALE	69

A WIFE OF NOBLE CHARACTER LINDSAY CRANDALL	71
AN ADAM OF MY OWN LINDSAY CRANDALL	75
BATHSHEBA AND THE KING LINDSAY CRANDALL	76
SUNSET YEARS SUZANNE RAE DESHCHIDN	78
TERMINAL JEFF NEWBERRY	79
A BODY'S LAMENT JEFF NEWBERRY	80
SUNLIGHT SHATTERED JEFF NEWBERRY	81
THING PSALM: THE POET'S ACT OF CONTRITION NINA FORSYTHE	82
WHAT WOULD JESUS WEAR JENNA RISANO	94
LITTLE GIRLS J. MARCUS WEEKLEY	103
PRODIGAL LYNN DOMINA	104
PREGNANT AND UNWED ON A SMALL CHRISTIAN CAMPUS IN KIRKLAND, WASHINGTON HOLLY CARTER	105
A SHORT HISTORY OF FAILURE TOM PAUL BIRD	122
THE JOB POEMS SARAH GAJKOWSKI-HILL	124
CREATOR, AUTHOR OF THE FOOL'S CANARD RICK MULLIN	127
IN ANOTHER UNIVERSE M. L. LIEBLER	128
NOTRE DAME ALIENE PYLANT	129
TETRAGRAMMATON MARC SHAW	130

COVER ART

THIS ISSUE'S COVER WAS BUILT BY TECHNICAL EDITOR COACH CULBERTSON. ORIGINAL PHOTO, "OUT OF THE DARK," PROVIDED BY GILLIAN TOWNSEND OF NORTH HAMPTON, UNITED KINGDOM. COVER TEXTURE PHOTOGRAPHY WAS PROVIDED BY CARMEN MARTINEZ OF CHICAGO, IL.

PLUS!

LOOK FOR A BONUS STORY, "SANCTUARY" BY LINDA GILMORE, AT THE END OF THE JOURNAL. YOU'LL ENJOY THE PREVIEW OF COACH'S MIDNIGHT DINER, THE GENRE ANTHOLOGY AVAILABLE NOW FROM CCPUBLISHING. CHECK IT OUT AT WWW.RELIEFJOURNAL.COM/STORE

FROM THE EDITOR'S DESK KIMBERLY CULBERTSON
EDITOR-IN-CHIEF

ONE MIGHT CALL IT THE EASY GOSPEL. After finding Christ, everything else should fall into place. Christians should feel clear-headed and fulfilled, never trapped or defeated. Though many would never use the words "easy gospel" to describe their message, the lesson is ingrained in church culture, where it is often implied that imperfect faith will bring immediate happiness. Perhaps that is why, so often, we become angry with God or question our own faith when life becomes unmanageable. How often is a lack of faith blamed for terrible circumstances—difficulties with health, finances, relationships, depression? And if a lack of faith is the universal cause for trouble, wouldn't it also stand to reason that enough faith would lead to a healthy, prosperous, love-filled, happy life? When I hear this message preached, I shudder; the easy gospel sets Christians up for bitterness and confusion.

I'm not discounting that faith does, in fact, sometimes make life easier. The Bible makes it clear that following God can move us toward blessing and generally keep our butts out of the fire. But it also does not exempt us from difficulty. Scripture claims that rain falls on the good land and the bad. Jesus warns that in this world we will have trouble, but (and this is a favorite line of mine) "Be of good cheer." It's like Jesus saying, "Hey, here comes the beat down—Smile!" And on a good day, we can. Because He is with us. The contentment Paul speaks of does not find its roots in the unwavering perfection of a quiet, simple life. Faith never promises to protect us from circumstance—from a terrible diagnosis, a natural disaster, a life altering accident, a financial blow, a betrayal. God may not always protect us from the fallout from sin—ours or someone else's. At times He intervenes, but sometimes He gives us strength for the battle or helps us pick up the pieces instead.

At other times though, faith gets dropped from the equation. Sometimes—because we haven't found God yet, because we're angry that He's let this (whatever *this* is) happen, because we're suddenly convinced that He doesn't give a damn, or sometimes, well, because faith just isn't an appealing coping mechanism—we seek answers, or at least pain management, in substance abuse, rage, affection, perfection, or depression. Sometimes it seems less risky to put away God,

FROM THE EDITOR'S DESK

with His miracles and healing, and in so doing put away expectation. When there is no hope, disappointment loses its sting. But the truth is that faith's intervention, our choice to take the risk and trust God, can mean the difference between an awful circumstance and a full downward spiral into a damaged life. When faith is part of the equation, though, we can walk away knowing Him and ourselves better. One way or another He will inevitably use the situation to reveal truth to us. And if we focus on Him, He will get us back on our feet—He's got a lot more to offer than a drink or a fight or a one-night stand.

In this issue, much of the work examines the intersection between faith, choice, and circumstance. Couples struggle in troubled marriages, choosing whether to fight for their connection or discard it, and their children face the consequences and make their own choices. A father pursues faith in the face of a child's death. One mother wrestles with the pain of her own orphaned past, another sacrifices a bond with her own child to protect a better future, and another bandages her soul as those around her cast judgment on her unwed pregnancy. Poverty, abuse, delinquency, and hypocrisy bubble up from childhood into the lives of men and women who are forced to reexamine and cope with their choices. Corporate executives find themselves stuck in a conference room while another gives clear vision from outside the window. A Muslim and a Christian navigate a friendship, skirting cultural limitations. A poet finds God in a tarot card reading. A worshiper recognizes God's vacancy in church culture and his own pious actions. The prodigal son, once welcomed home, finds that his guilt is magnified and sin is still seductive.

In each issue, we have chosen to showcase a piece from each genre by honoring the author with the "Editor's Choice Award." In Issue Four, we offer our congratulations to Christopher Fisher for his essay "Scars," C. A. Hasselbalch for her poem "An Italian Restaurant in Dominion," and Edmund de Chasca for his story "Epithalamium." Each of these pieces addresses the theme of choice and circumstance in marriage from a different angle.

Our lives, and, as authors, the lives of our characters, are a steady stream of circumstance. It is tempting to define people by what they have experienced, but any good author will know that true character is defined by the choices made in response. God, the author of our existence, certainly does.

HERE AT RELIEF, we are headed into a period of recalibration. After a full year of publication—four journals and two anthologies—we've discovered what is and is not working and more than a few ways to improve. With this in mind, there will be a short delay in our production schedule as we upgrade our submission system, web presence, and publication process. We'll be back to our regularly scheduled program in February 2008 with Volume Two, Issue One of *Relief*. In the meantime, you can tune in to the *Best of Relief* anthology, due in November, and also to our website for regular updates and new content. To get a more specific idea of what's ahead, just flip the page to Coach's Corner, where he'll lay out our goals with Coach's famous candor.

As always, thank you for choosing *Relief*. Your support allows us to continue and allows Christian writers a new kind of venue. May you find perspective and enjoyment in these pages.

COACH'S CORNER COACH CULBERTSON

HELLO FRIENDS, COACH HERE WITH BIG NEWS.

As Kimberly mentioned, we have changed our production schedule in order to make room for some important changes. Issue 5 (which technically will be Volume 2, Issue 1) will be released in Februrary 2008. In the meantime, we'll be taking some time to use what we've learned in the last year to improve our processes. Here's a short version of what's happening in the next couple of months:

1. We will be moving to a new printing company that will allow us more flexibility and more distribution options.

2. A completely new web site will be released which we've been affectionately calling Relief 2.0. The Online Submissions System is getting an overhaul and will be integrated into the Relief Writers Network, which will improve accessibility for authors.

4. The Relief Writers Network will be smoothed out, refined, and properly integrated into the ReliefJournal.com site.

5. *Coach's Midnight Diner* will be getting its own Web presence.

THERE WILL BE A FEW MORE IMPROVEMENTS AS WELL, but these are the major highlights.

We're going to be reinstating our regular blogging on the front page, chronicling our improvement processes and pouring out some insights into writing, reality, and publishing. Thanks for hanging in with us as we lay the foundations for the future of *Relief*. Stay tuned for more exciting news at www.reliefjournal.com!

Your friendly neighborhood system administrator,
Coach Culbertson
Technical Editor | *Relief: A Quarterly Christian Expression*

RELIEF | A QUARTERLY CHRISTIAN EXPRESSION
CONGRATULATES THE WINNERS OF ITS
EDITOR'S CHOICE AWARDS

CREATIVE NONFICTION
CHRISTOPHER FISHER
SCARS

POETRY
C. A. HASSELBALCH
AN ITALIAN RESTAURANT

FICTION
EDMUND DE CHASCA
EPITHALAMIUM

SCARS CHRISTOPHER FISHER

I. Strangers

Here's a dare. Next time you're out in a crowd, pick a spot to sit, or just stand still. Then watch, really look at the faces of the strangers who pass you by. Try to ignore the things you'd normally notice first—eyes, hair, lips. You want to focus, instead, on the skin. Look deep, right down to the lines and wrinkles.

Now, find one face—just one—that doesn't carry a scar.

I've been doing this off and on for eighteen years in airports and shopping malls, libraries and church auditoriums. I've never found one. And I don't think you can, either. Oh, you might have to look hard, but the scar is there.

Every face is scarred, and behind each scar is a story.

It's the story behind the scar that has always fascinated me. Sometimes after noticing a particularly interesting one, I'll give in and ask a stranger how he got his. If you're polite about it, most people are more than willing to tell. The stories are almost always of childhood injury—a fall from the front porch, a bike wreck. I guess we all have to kiss the dirt a few times before we learn what hands are for. Or maybe young skin scars easier.

My scar is a pencil-thin line, barely noticeable, tracing my left cheekbone. It has faded through the years, so much that unless I pointed it out, you might not even notice it. I once worked up a story—in case someone asked—about a pack of wild dogs and a barbed wire fence. No one ever asked, so I never got to tell it. The story I'll tell you is different, though. Not as exciting as seven Cujos chasing me into a fence, but pretty good. And true, too.

II. A Gift from Dad

When I was a boy, I lived with my parents and two sisters on an Oklahoma farm. This was not a *real* farm—we didn't grow crops or breed livestock for a living—but we had several farm animals. Pets, actually. By the time I was twelve we had owned at one time or another four horses, two goats, one large sow, a couple dozen rabbits, a flock of ducks, and maybe fifty chickens.

Let's talk about chickens. Chickens begin as eggs, of course. They bust out of their shells all smelly and sticky. Not a pretty sight. Within a few hours, though, their feathers are clean and fluffy and yellow. All baby chicks are yellow. At least that's the way I remember it.

One winter night when I was six, Dad brought home a box of chicks from the feed store. My sisters and I crowded around him, nudging in close as he set the box on the kitchen floor and hung a lamp over its side. Inside, seven or eight clean, yellow chicks huddled together, chirping under the warm light.

Whenever a new litter of puppies or kittens arrived, it was my childhood custom to pick a favorite—usually the runt, or the one with the spot or the longest ears. Looking over the tiny balls of feather, I found picking a chick would be difficult. They were all identical.

I leaned over the box for several minutes, crinkling my nose at the smell of cardboard and chicken crap baking in the heat of the lamp. When I finally reached inside, the chicks scurried away—all but one. I picked it up and lifted it to my face. It chirped, then pecked hard at my nose.

"It kissed me," I said with a smile.

My younger sister, Amy, asked, "What are you going to name him?" I peeked between the chick's legs but saw no evidence that it was a him. Years later, I would hear of a man who made six figures sexing chickens for poultry farms—two hundred thousand dollars a year for peeking between the legs of baby chicks. To a seven-year-old child, however (and to most normal adults for that matter) there is no visible difference between a baby rooster and a baby hen. In the end, I ignored the usual rules of observation and trusted Amy's intuition. The chick would be a him, and I named him Sunshine, for his bright, yellow feathers.

III. Little Sister

I can't speak of scars without mentioning my sister, Amy. There was a time, way back there, when we were very close, but somewhere around the age of five, probably due to my constant bullying, Amy got very mean and very tough. She could whip all of my younger male cousins, and she could even whip me from time to time, if I turned my back on her. Half the scars on my body can be attributed to Amy. My scalp alone she split with a lamp, a steel pipe, and even a shovel.

She was tough.

I was fifteen and Amy was thirteen when Dad left Mom and moved to the city. My older sister, Kim, was married by then. So only Mom, Amy, and I were left on the farm. The three of us took the news like a shovel over the head. And though that blow left no physical mark, the emotional scars went deep. Mom lost her mind for the next two years. She went through counseling and overdosed on sleeping pills a couple of times. I claimed God as father, in the absence of my own, and locked myself in my bedroom like a monk in his cell. And Amy, that tough little girl, began to look more and more each day like a cancer victim. She wore the wound on her face like a steel frown behind a thin, plastic smile.

IV. JESUS AND ZEN

I have this friend who speaks of Christ, Tao, and Zen Enlightenment in the same sentence. He calls himself a Christian mystic, but not a Christian. "Modern Christianity is a neutered religion. An emasculated faith. It's Christ with all smiles and no scars."

Being men, we speak often of women. "There's a reason they're called the weaker sex, you know. And it's not meant as an insult. Just ask any woman if she would rather be strong or pretty. Strength is the pride of a man; beauty is that of a woman."

I've seen what he's talking about. Men wear their scars like badges, pointing them out with pride. *Look! I have been bloodied in battle, and I am still here.* I've never felt uncomfortable asking a man about his scars, because I know he *wants* to tell. But with women . . .

Women cover their scars with make-up.

V. A GOOD BIRD

I spent a lot of time with Sunshine those first few weeks. As the other chicks ate grain from the bottom of their box, I fed Sunshine from my hand. I set him on my shoulder and took him for walks around the house while he nibbled at my earlobe. I lay on the carpet as he scratched around on my chest. Sometimes, I would even sing for him. He in turn would peck playfully at my nose.

Weeks passed. The days grew longer. Trees began to bud. Time for the chicks to go outside, Mom said. That spring I learned to ride a bicycle without the training wheels, and our Doberman bitch had puppies. I didn't spend much time with Sunshine after that. A chicken has nothing on a puppy or a bicycle.

Sunshine, who turned out to be a rooster after all, didn't mind my absence, for it was about this time that he discovered the hens. Full grown, he still had most of the yellow feathers for which he had been named, making him stand out next to the black and white hens. Occasionally, he would jump on one of their backs and flap his wings wildly.

"Stop fighting with her, Sunshine!" I would shout. Being the good bird he was, he hopped off and pecked at the ground while I turned to chase a puppy across the yard.

By the following autumn, my rooster and I were no longer on friendly terms. He fought more and more with the hens and no longer obeyed my commands. Once, I tried to feed him out of my hand and he just squawked and flew off across the yard.

I knew what the problem was. He was angry about the puppy. He'd been jealous of that puppy all along. Even after all the puppies—including my favorite—were sold at the end of summer, Sunshine held a grudge. Mom said it wasn't good to hold grudges, that I should forgive my sisters if they did something against me. So I decided the bird should be the one to apologize, and I would not speak to him until he did.

One afternoon, while I was playing under the big elm that shaded our house, I noticed Sunshine strutting with the hens nearby. I paid no attention, shunning him as usual. Suddenly, I heard a swooshing sound and looked up to find Sunshine hovering right in front of me.

I'd never seen a chicken hover, and never have since. But there he was, flapping his wings in a steady, graceful beat—floating effortlessly in place, just inches from my face.

VI. Scar Face

I have a rather old face. Not wrinkled, really. Not yet. Just serious—even angry—and a little worn. Always has been. I've never had trouble buying liquor thanks to this face, though that might have more to do with my facial hair.

I started shaving at thirteen. At the time, I was afraid my family, and especially Amy, would tease me about it. So I didn't tell them. For two years. Eventually, the whiskers became too thick to hide, like sixty grit sandpaper that grew back every eight hours. I let it grow out for a week then told Dad I wanted to start shaving. He held my chin in his hand, turning my face in the light. "Maybe it *is* time we get you some razors."

The idea seemed silly to me, the two of us in front of the mirror wearing white, foamy beards, and me feigning ignorance as he showed me how it was done. But the next day, Dad came home from the drug store, handed me a pack of Bics and a can of Barbasol, then sat down in front of the TV.

It's funny. There wasn't a thing he could have taught me. But I resented him for not trying.

VII. Sunshine

Sunshine hovered in front of me, and it was all so clear what the rooster wanted. He was coming to make amends, to apologize for behaving so selfishly. A smile stretched across my face, and in my heart, I forgave him that instant. In a tone of welcome and wonder, I said, "Sunshine!"

Sunshine. That's all I got out before he stretched out his claw and dragged a spur across my face. I screamed, horrified at the sting of pain and betrayal. The rooster squawked and flew off over my head. With one hand to my cheek—where the scar remains to this day—I turned to see him flapping clumsily across the yard. He landed near the hens and started scratching at the dirt as if nothing had happened.

My vision blurred with tears, and I wailed, "Maw-muh!" Mom came running out the door and, seeing my face wet with tears and blood, shrieked, "What happened? What happened?" I ran to meet her and latched on, pressing my bleeding face into her belly. All I could do was point and sob, "Sunshine, Mama! Sunshine!"

Mom brought me inside and cleaned me up. The scratch had already stopped bleeding, so she put peroxide on it, but not a Band-Aid; it was long, but not at all deep. She gave me a cookie and some juice, and fifteen minutes later I was outside playing again.

VIII. Of A Boy

Strength is the pride of a man. And of a boy. Especially a boy.

I remember one night, just before the divorce, Amy and I were in Tulsa at an outdoor concert, right on the banks of the Arkansas River. Dad and Mom were also there, a couple of seats down. Some man, half-drunk and half-stoned, sat down next to us and tried to sell us a joint. Dad overheard the proposition and knocked the guy on his ass before we could even "just say no." I'll never forget Dad's face as he watched that drunk cower off to the other side of the amphitheater, the hardness radiating like waves of heat from his eyes, the muscles in his jaw flexing and releasing in time with the music. Even as the roar of the band and the murmur of the crowd swarmed around me and echoed back off the water, I thought I heard Dad's teeth grinding against each other, like the crunching of bones. This is my favorite memory of Dad, the moment he was hell-bent on shedding blood to protect us. I have never been so proud of my father.

A few months after that night, Mom and Dad separated. One morning soon after, I rode into town with my Grandfather, Mom's father.

Talk about *scars*. Grandpa was a walking scar, and the strongest man I've ever known. He worked thirty years in a steel casting plant—a place closer to hell than any I've seen. His arms, neck, and face were freckled with tiny white scars, where molten metal had popped onto his skin like bacon grease. But he never complained. He was just happy to keep his kids fed and in shoes.

Driving me to town, Grandpa talked about the separation, how bad it was, how hard it was going to be for me. "You're the man of the house now, Chris. Whether you like it or not. You're gonna have to look after your Mom and sister."

Shoulders back, chin up, I nodded in silent agreement. I was a man at fifteen. Grandpa said so.

IX. SUNSHINE

By the time Dad came home, I had almost forgotten about the fight with Sunshine. I forgave the bird. But it could not end so simply. Dad took one look at my face then shot a glance to my mother. "What happened to him?"

Mom shook her head. "That damn rooster flogged him."

Dad inspected the scratch on my cheek, holding my chin in his hand and turning my face into the light. I felt the heat coming off his eyes and heard the grinding of his teeth as he stared at the long, red line. And I knew even at that innocent age that something terrible, something violent was about to happen. He looked me in the eye and said, "Go help your mother peel some potatoes."

That phrase apparently had some secret meaning to my mother, who nodded slowly and led me to the kitchen. She put me at the table and set a peeler, a paper sack, and a big pot of potatoes down in front of me. But my eyes followed Dad, who walked into the bedroom and came out with his .22 pistol. He walked around a corner into the living room. I heard the front door open. Then shut.

I looked up at Mom, but she wouldn't look me in the eyes.

"Kim and Amy can help too," she said, then went off to find them.

As soon as she left the kitchen, I dropped the potato peeler and rushed to the window. A moment later my jaw dropped open.

Dad stomped toward the barn, holding Sunshine upside down by the feet as the rooster flapped its wings wildly, trying to escape. When they were a good distance from the house,

Dad stopped. Taking Sunshine's head in his free hand, he twisted it all the way around about three times. Then he took the pistol out of a pocket and shot the bird in the head—twice.

When Mom and my sisters returned to the kitchen, I was back at the table shedding tears and potato peels into the paper sack.

X. Man Of The House

The Christian God is a god of love, as you may have heard, a Father who loves all his sons and daughters. But that's not the whole truth. The same book that says God is Love also tells us that He hates. This is only one of those contradictions in scripture that has had theologians arguing for the past two thousand years. I confess I'm not comfortable with the idea of a God who hates. Who could be? But if you spend as many hours hiding in an open Bible as I did after Dad left, you'll find it's undeniable. If you are to believe the Bible, there are at least forty-five things God hates. And one of these, with few exceptions, is divorce. "Putting away," the prophet Malachi calls it, which in many divorces is an excellent description, calling to mind the way you might carelessly reshelf a book after you've laid bare all its secrets, studied all its naked pages, gotten out of it all you wanted.

When a marriage ends the way my parents' did, when one spouse just puts away the other after more than twenty years, it's as devastating as throwing a live grenade on the living room rug and running out the door. The one left behind gets all the shrapnel, along with anyone else who happens to be in the house, like the children. And those scars are for life.

I didn't really need to read the Bible to know the evils of "putting away." All I had to do was watch what the separation did to my mother. The loss of emotional control. The constant crying. The pulling at her hair—I mean literally ripping it from her scalp. Living through that, I could not imagine a God who could smile on such a thing. I still cannot. But if Mom wasn't proof enough, I had my little sister as further evidence.

Amy's scar became more pronounced each year, despite her efforts to hide it. It was painful watching her hurt like that. I tried my best to help her. But, unfortunately, my idea of help was reading her my own list of the things she was doing which God hated. As you can imagine, my judgment and Sunday school solutions did nothing to heal her wound. So she sought other cures. Sex, drugs, alcohol . . . sex. Sex especially.

I worked all through high school, and one rainy winter night I came home late. Mom was out—she was gone a lot around that time—but Amy's car was parked outside. As I walked inside, shivering and wet, Amy came out of her bedroom and shut the door, her back firmly against it.

"Hey. How was work?" she asked.

"Fine," I said. She must have really thought I was stupid. "I'm gonna make a sandwich," I said, then turned to the kitchen. She darted into her room and shut the door behind her. I waited twenty seconds, then walked down the hall, opened her door, and asked, "Do you want a sandwi—" That last word trailed off as I saw what was going on.

Some kid I had never seen lay on the far side of Amy's tousled bed, pulling on his pants. Amy stood at the raised window, fighting to get the screen off so the boy could sneak out. The three of us froze solid, waiting, wondering what I would do. I think they were certain I would lose it, grab him by the hair and throw him through the window myself. And that's what I *felt* like doing. Only not through the window. Through the wall. But I could see this was no case of rape—not even statutory. The kid looked at least a year younger than Amy.

I held it in and said with a steely voice, "Get your clothes on and get the hell out of my house."

As it turned out, the boy didn't even drive. Amy had brought him to the house in her car. She offered to take him home. "No," I said, not trusting her. "I'll take him." Amy insisted on coming along, and it's a good thing she did. Her presence may have spared him a few scars of his own.

Not a word was spoken the whole drive, apart from an occasional "Turn here." When I pulled up in front of his house, he got out quickly. I put the car in park and followed him, leaving Amy alone in the back seat. I stood with that boy in the freezing rain for fifteen minutes—me talking, him nodding emphatically. It was a long lecture, but basically all I said was, "If I ever see you around my sister again I'll rip your head off and hide it where it will never be found."

Never saw him again.

The drive home—with Amy—was quieter than the drive there. I couldn't think of anything to say to her. And I knew one of my sermons would accomplish nothing. I may have scared this one away, but she would have another boyfriend in a week. All I could think during that long drive was how unfair it was for me to even be in this position. It was not my job. I wasn't her father. I wasn't even a man, despite all my proud pretending. I was just an eighteen-year-old kid, wishing his father was there. I needed him, and I loved him. But I also hated.

XI. To Give Than To Receive

Hurt people hurt people.

I hate to admit it, but after three long years as the "man of the house," I gave up on Amy. I had school. I had work. I had grass to cut in the summer and wood to split in the winter, and I had no more time or breath to preach to Amy about how she should live. She never listened to my sermons anyway. So I "handed her over to the devil" like I was taught to do with reprobates and hopeless causes.

What a thing to do to your own blood.

Still, I managed to enjoy my senior year. I was an actor in high school, and a notorious prankster. There was a cast party one night, after we finished the last of seven showings of *A Midsummer Night's Dream*. The whole cast was there, from Oberon to the very least of his fairies. But the one I remember now is Steven—a quiet, slightly effeminate junior. A good kid. He played Snug and the Lion. We were all high on stage adrenaline, eager to do something crazy. Someone suggested we go hiking through the woods in the dark. Oooh, scary! Maybe it was to them, but I was used to being in the forest at night. We set out into the dark, and after ten minutes of watching these city kids trip over roots and swing flashlight beams through the treetops, I had an idea for a prank that would have made Robin Goodfellow proud.

Quietly, I split from the group, turned off my flashlight, and crept a good distance away. Once I was far enough so they couldn't hear, I sprinted through the dark woods in a wide circle, coming around in front of them. Then I stopped and, panting from the run, waited for their approach. As soon as I saw the nervous beams flickering ahead, I grabbed a dead branch, stood up, and yelled, "Y'all kids get off my land!"

They ran, flashlights bobbing in rhythm with their retreat. I pursued, yelling the whole way and beating the stick on tree trunks. My blood rushed. My head filled with an endorphin-charged high, a furious exhilaration that felt like fist fighting, cliff diving, and French kissing all at the same time. I caught up with them in a clearing, where I threw myself on the ground in laughter. They didn't know whether to kiss me or kill me, so they took turns cursing me and laughing at themselves.

That's when I noticed Steven. He stood quiet, away from the group, his hand pressed to his face. The white T-shirt he always wore under his costume now sported a black oak-leaf design on the front. When I turned my flashlight on him, the black leaf turned red.

They had come to a barbed wire fence; that's why they had stopped in the clearing. Steven ran smack into the top wire and caught a barb just a centimeter under his right eye and didn't say a word to anyone. You can never tell just by looking who the strong ones are.

Steven took seven stitches that night. Within a couple of months, the scar healed remarkably—a gray thread the only evidence of the gash that almost took his eye. But for those weeks while it healed, I couldn't look Steven in the face. I felt sick each time I saw that swollen pink scar, convinced he would live out his years disfigured because of my foolishness, queasy with the knowledge that, at the moment I was having the time of my life, his tender skin was learning the cruelty of rusted steel.

XII. A Good Bird

Mom plucked Sunshine in the kitchen sink, dropping fistfuls of bright yellow feathers into the sack of potato peels. She cut his body into pieces, rolled the pieces in flour, and then dropped them in a pan of hot grease. Sunshine popped and sizzled in the grease, and I slouched off to my bedroom to cry.

Soon the house filled with the smell of Sunshine frying in the kitchen, and to my shame, my mouth watered even as the tears flowed. I vowed then that I would not eat. How could I even think of it? It would be obscene, even cannibalistic. When the table was set, Mom called us into the kitchen. I choked down my tears, set my jaw, and took my seat at the table.

For half an hour I sat with my arms folded and watched my family feast on mashed potatoes, peas, corn, hot biscuits, and fried Sunshine. My stomach rumbled. My mouth watered. Icy cold sweat rose up on my forehead and, to my horror, I saw my own trembling hand reach across the table. A voice inside my head screamed, "Fight it! Don't give in! He was your friend!" But I was young and unaccustomed to such powerful temptation. Despite all my efforts to resist, my fingers grasped a warm, crispy drumstick and pulled it toward my plate.

XIII. Beauty for Ashes

I wonder what my Zen friend would say about my eating Sunshine. "You absorbed your enemy and used his energy to heal the wound he gave you." Something like that. He would be right, except for one detail. The rooster was also my friend, once.

But Sunshine's energy went far and the wound healed well. You wouldn't even see it unless I pointed it out. I hardly see it myself anymore, only when I'm shaving. But I love to see it. It reminds me of a time when I knew Dad loved me and would fight to protect me.

I love him for killing that bird.

And that other wound? I still feel the sting from time to time. When it comes, I let it. I pray. I cry. I write as if great drops of blood fell from my brow. And in the fevered exhaustion that follows, I find that the pain is eased—absorbed. The scar is still there, deep down. But I don't wear it on my face.

Amy does. Her scars have faded some, but like mine, they have a funny way of coming back. When it gets really bad, she has a dinner of prescription painkillers, followed by a vacation in a private hospital. This has happened three times, I think.

She made her own choices, I know, but there is a stinging suspicion that just maybe I could have done more. I could have refrained from judging and tried to understand what watching Dad walk out the door did to her. I could have at least spared one slap for that boy in her bedroom, and maybe a black-eyed ex-boyfriend could have been for her what a dead rooster became for me, proof that someone loved her enough to protect her. If nothing else, I could have simply wept with her, which might have been the thing she needed most. Instead, I played the Pharisee and watched her drown.

Sometimes it makes me sick to look at her, as sick as I felt when I looked at that scar on Steven's face. And I hope Dad feels the same way when he sees his daughter. I hope he still loves her enough to hurt for her. And to *hurt* for her.

If I had the hands of Christ, I would erase the hard years, wipe the worried lines from my sister's face like chalk from a blackboard, and every plastic surgeon in Beverly Hills would stand in awe. She would be that beautiful.

XIV. One He Never Gave

When I was a boy, almost a man, I came home from school to see that Dad had come to visit. He did this occasionally, after the separation and before the divorce. Just dropped by to talk to Mom. I didn't know then what they had left to talk about, though now I think I do.

Anyway, Mom and I got into it over something—God only knows what. Before long, we were screaming at each other, while Dad sat passively at the table. I've already said that Mom was insane at this point, and it's no exaggeration. She started swinging her fists at my face, intent on bringing blood. I blocked her blows, but she kept coming, backing me into a wall. I had to do something to stop her before she really did hurt me.

I grabbed her wrists. That's all I did. Grabbed her wrists and pushed her back a couple of feet.

Dad was up and on me in a beat. He snatched a fistful of my shirt and shoved me backward over a chair, pinning me upside down. His other fist came up, cocked and ready to slam into my mouth.

I'll never forget what went through my head at that moment, suspended in the grip of violence. Sure I was scared. Scared to death. My eyes watered under the heat from his stare. My whole frame melted at the sight of that flexing jaw, the noise of those grinding teeth. Still, part of me could have cried with joy, realizing that he still loved her. Thank God, he still loved her! But Dad's face relaxed. He lowered his fist. He let go of me and turned away.

I wish he had hit me.

Hard.

I would have worn the scar like a medal.

AN ITALIAN RESTAURANT IN DOMINION CAROL ANN HASSELBALCH

Sanguine spirits, vapid wine
The night wore on while we talked respectfully
    of our modus vivendi,
Our compromise on behalf of our biological dependent, the son,
still in training pants who had now gained a stutter thanks to our selfishness

And still, the thick-fingered accordionist, with eyes closed
played what sounded like music from *La Dolce Vita*

fickle organ, bloody bag,
it pumps 7,500 liters a day
but cannot cover the slightest of sin
So we drink on in Holy Communion with death

The red and white checkered table cloth beneath us
The single carnation in a glass Coke bottle, the soft glow of the candle
Unable to swallow the past, incapable of forgiving the future
while the lamb on our plates, untouched, grows cold.

EPITHALAMIUM EDMUND DE CHASCA

She laughed to herself over the irony of it as she closed the pearl buttons on her suit. In an era when few of the young people could legitimately wear white she, older now than their mothers, had put on this gray woolen dress because women her age did not wear white. How many times had she received their invitations, two or three years after they graduated, at first addressed to Miss Frances Atkins, then Ms., and she had bought the gift and played the role of the well-wisher knowing that for most of them white was a mockery. Now, when it was her turn, she and Walter had agreed it would be just the two of them and the lawyer in a downtown office building. Which was fine. Disappointment had come and gone early in her life. She only hoped Walter would not be let down by her. He was so excited, like a boy.

She took her place in her orange wing chair that faced the television she had come home to for so many years and waited for the cab. Walter had insisted that he not see her on this day until they were both in the room before the Justice. She took a last look around her rooms. The horn of the cab tooted. She hefted her small overnight bag—Walter had taken the suitcase yesterday—and went to meet it.

He studied his list one last time: Confirm room reservation and AARP discount, traveler's checks, cash for Justice, cash for tips, rings, medications. He surveyed the master bedroom where his mother had languished for over a decade. He and Frances had redecorated it, following mostly her suggestions. Now it would be their room, their home. He could not make time stand still, but he could control it, make those days leading up to the day perfect, as much as a human possibly could, so that for once the outside world would match the radiance within. Even to the point of when he clipped his nails, three days before so that there was the tiniest crescent. Had his hair cut ten days before. The navy blue suit cleaned but removed from its wrapping so that it would not smell of naphtha. His shoes still new, but broken in.

The body was another matter. He'd worked out a plan with his doctor and would stick to it. Beyond that, he had no control. Eliminate the blood pressure pill that morning but take the one for his tachycardia. Drop the heavy painkiller that sometimes tied him up and substitute Tylenol. He'd wanted to skip the Dyazide for a couple of days since it affected blood flow, but the doctor had shaken his head so they'd compromised: this morning only, he could miss his dosage. Now he was ready for his day, his one day.

Midday light from the ninth-floor window of the law office shone on the faces of Walter and Frances as they stood before Michael Kaplan, a junior partner in Walter's firm. When he began to close the blinds, Walter requested that he leave them open. He wanted the room full of light. By angling themselves away from the desk they could keep it from blinding them. The attorney noticed a scuff mark on his shoes, so polished they gleamed. He spat on his fingers and wiped it away. The couple did not notice. They acted as if their world was beginning. He recalled his own wedding day. Even fifteen years ago it had cost twelve thousand dollars, the band, over a hundred guests. He'd had so much champagne, the wedding night was a fiasco, not that it mattered . . . their actual wedding night had come long before.

Under the authority of the state, he pronounced Walter Sturgis and Frances Atkins man and wife. Then he winced as Walter kissed her on the mouth. The suddenness of the act, like some animal striking, unnerved him. Who did they think they were? Walter must be close to retirement age, his "bride" not that far behind. Granted, Sturgis had a certain distinction, though he belonged to a different era with his wing tips and suspenders and hair combed straight back with that tonic smeared on it. And the schoolteacher, to her credit, had kept her figure. But their behavior was unseemly. They were infringing on an area they should keep out of, that still partly belonged to him.

Frances could hear the television from behind the closed bathroom door even though the water was running. Bless him, it was so loud, she would have to learn to put a piece of cotton or tissue in her ears. She would encourage him to visit a hearing specialist and if he wanted to put it off, that was all right too. She lowered herself into the aloe bubble bath. The day had gone well, except for the exit Walter had missed on the way to the resort. The hotel was lovely, the room lovely, the meal lovely. And now . . . a tear dropped into the froth. Once again she saw the moon reflected on the lake in Minnesota where they had taken a family vacation and Carl was running his fingertips up the back of her legs, pleading with her, and she had said, "There won't be anything left." Now, a lifetime later, it was still left. She cried, not because she could not summon the feeling from that night, but because she had saved herself so long for this good man, this Walter. More tears fell. Just as well to get the crying over with now. He might misinterpret it later.

Walter's heart pounded. He wondered if his blood pressure was up. He could have brought his cuff along, taken it now while Frances was in the bath. He laughed at the absurdity of it. He had a good laugh, one that came from deep within, yet was high-pitched for such a big man. He did not have to sneak in his blood pressure checks. They would have no secrets. He turned off the television. He'd only had it on to give her some privacy. He had his over his pajamas, some resort magazine on his lap which he hadn't even glanced at. Unable to hear any sound from the bathroom, he grew alarmed and walked to the door. He could hear the faint lap of water. She would be a few minutes at least. He knelt by the side of the bed and buried his head in his hands.

They lay in bed. The hallways were silent. Everyone on their wing was in for the night. A lamp glowed in the corner of the room. Frances rested her head on Walter's shoulder.

"It's not your fault," Frances said.

"Yes it is. You wanted to see the doctor and I talked you out of it."

"I'm not sure she could have helped. Maybe it's just nerves that tense me up. Maybe tomorrow will be different."

"No. If it's that painful for you we should wait until we get back and you see Doctor Gorde."

Frances kissed his cheek. "Always so thoughtful." They were silent, then she said, "I had a perfect wedding day."

Walter patted her hand. "We can try the spa tomorrow. Or go into town if you feel like shopping. I understand they have a lot of antique stores."

"Yes, we can see how we feel. Travel is always such a strain. Do you want me to get the light?"

"I will."

He half-rolled out of bed to spare his back. He removed the blood pressure pill and swallowed it. He switched off the light and got back into bed.

Frances yawned. "I love you, darling. Sweet dreams."

"I love you Frances."

She turned onto her side away from him. Walter remained on his back, his eyes wide open. Frances was right; it had been a perfect day. They had crossed over into that white circle in which they would be contained forever. Nothing outside could get in and clutter it. They were married and this was his wife beside him, now breathing with the heavy rhythms of a dream-filled sleep.

FINDING THE RING DAVID BEDSOLE

Between the row
and the reconciliation
her ring dropped from her finger.

It was almost as if
the little gold band knew
that discord is impossible

when you're both on your knees
searching together
for what you promised.

MY THERAPIST SAYS I NEED TO LEARN GRACE DAVID BEDSOLE

When young, you will think the world balanced
on the sharpened tip of a pencil, changes tracked
to the decimal point. It will seem as if time inches
rather than unfurls, and that love is sure as gravity.

Older, you learn the answer to everyone's question:
good enough? is not always *yes* or *no*, sometimes *no, but*—
and in that very *but* rides the long energy of grace,
where things are more like improvisation than arithmetic,

where the moon pulls shuttles toward her in welcome,
and everyone you wronged is winking fondly
behind your back. This conspiracy of mercy baffles
more than heals, and yet something rings clear

in the way her body adjusts to yours, tiny surrenders
in dance, blast of rain seconds too late to ruin the day,
the way everything makes room for you, only you, mismatched,
forgotten part, and grace the secret grease of a grinding world.

PRISON WORK DAVID BEDSOLE

I claim no knowledge of criminal life,
construct my motion like links on a chain,
am quashed. It's funny; to talk to my wife,
you'd think I consist of legs and a brain,
a moving recital of heady tripe.
The truth is this: if my heart were released—
cooling in my ribcage, you know the type—
this hardened offender, pure hell on police,
would dump my skull's contents out at my feet,
hotwire my legs and demand cigarettes,
trick out my penis, and head for the streets.
For now, this poem is as close as it gets,
an obscene gesture from a bored inmate.
As prison work goes, it beats license plates.

WINDOW WASHER S. R. KOVACOVIC

The window washer never painted a sunset such as this
    —ox blood red dashed on cerulean oil—
or the majestic city of brick and mortar
    dotted with lights
    that smear with rain.
These high rise cells
have seen the worst of humanity's best thinking
huddled under veneered oak desks
and conference room tables
with sirens wrapped and singing lovely melodies
around his waterlogged calves.
    These rooms have been targeted
    by the Competitor.
    These rooms are the best of what
    the American dream has got to offer.
These rooms, with their filthy windows,
will plummet to the sub-cellar
where the boiler spits and burps
lamenting fire.
    But, behold the squeegee,
    the humble rag—a white flag
    waving from the washer's back pocket.
He plows the grime within and without
in pretzel snail paths before washing them away
with the wavering cloth and the Baptismal midst of Windex.
    Pulling a cord, he hoists himself up
    to the next floor
    for the next window
    of the next room,
never remaining long enough

to see us emerge like Neanderthals half idiotic
from under our desks and behind
locked doors
to bathe our pale and sunken faces
in the forsaken sunlight
of a beautiful day.

    Alas! We are sober.
    Alas! We are awake.
    Alas! We have been saved
        so we may save.

THE ATLANTIC D. S. MARTIN

I remember dissecting the dark mysteries of theology
one night   on a Florida beach in my youth
the Atlantic breathing as though alive
    my friends & I having followed
    the red ribbon of I-75
    all the way from Detroit to the coast
It was as though   by our free will   we were predestined
to oversimplify the vastness we faced
to participate in the cartography of the Holy Ghost
    experiencing the salty taste
    the wind stirring high in the palm trees
    & the joy of the shore   as our strength
Essential   though like a futile attempt to embrace
the sea   to put that entire ocean in a bottle
to be slipped into a message

SWIMMERS INTO CLEANNESS LEAPING ALAN ACKMANN

Now, God be thanked who has matched us with His hour
And caught our youth, and wakened us from sleeping,
With hand made sure, clear eye, and sharpened power,
To turn, as swimmers into cleanness leaping.
 —Rupert Brooke, *Peace*

ON THE MORNING OF AUGUST 27, 1922, when my friends and I scrambled down the cliffs of La Quebrada, Acapulco was little more than a trading post, a place of huts and lean-tos. The road connecting us with Mexico City, which would make the city bloom, was years away, so for the moment Acapulco got its romance (and its legends) from one person who we'd woken up to see. There were four of us, that morning, stumbling through the brush. Marco was first, and flanked by Julio, who was wheezing with the exertion. I followed Julio, and behind me, lifting up her skirt, was Maria. Like most things we did, this had been Maria's idea, and as we stared up at the cliff tops, forty meters high, I remember thinking that the stories that we had heard were simply rumors, passed by older kids. But then, as the sun worked its way across Mexico, we saw him—silhouetted—and his shadow stretched across the Bay. He gazed out at the ocean. His name was C. H. Driscoll. And in a moment, we were certain, he would jump.

Driscoll removed his pants, and Julio muttered, "I'll be damned. Will you go on and look at that?" Marco and I chuckled. Then, as Driscoll raised his arms, his shadow on the waves grew wings, then sucked itself towards land as he jumped, and slipped below the surface. Where we were, we heard no splash. "That's a hell of a drop." Julio muttered, "I hope he makes it, huh?"

"He made it," Maria replied.

Only now, years later, as I pack a light suitcase and leave Mexico City for Acapulco, can I begin to understand why Driscoll jumped. But at the time, I remember thinking that it hadn't looked that hard. Why, I could even do it too, if I had wanted.

I could do it too.

"I HEARD HE WAS A SOLDIER." Julio said later, as we drank beer by the abandoned Spanish fort. "I heard he came over from fighting in the war. You hear about people breaking over there, losing their reason. Jumping off a cliff like that? Don't take much reason."

The truth was, no one knew who Driscoll was, where he was from. Occasionally he did some hired work, aligning clay tile on a roof or furrowing a rich man's sugar fields. But beyond this Driscoll was a mystery. As I leaned against one of the fort's forgotten canons, I was listening to Marco and Julio, but I was looking at Maria, and beyond her, past the jungles, toward the cliffs of La Quebrada. Maria tucked a wayward hair behind her ear. She had said little since the jump—although she never spoke much, really—and I thought about how, recently, Driscoll had begun to look at her.

"I don't see what kind of tragedy can make a man leap off a cliff like that." I said.

"Well, why don't we just ask him?" Marco quipped.

"It's not our business."

"Oh, come on. We've watched the man jump naked off a cliff, eh? That's a bond. What's the trouble, Jose? You shy?"

"I want to meet him." Julio popped in. "Why don't we ask him out one night? He never talks to no one."

"Not a good idea," I said.

"Why not?"

Maria said, "I'd like to meet him too."

We all stopped then, and nodded. Maria was two years older than us, with chestnut eyes of stubborn, Aztec pride. She was a politician's daughter. Now and then Marco and I (or Julio, if he'd been drinking) would place a hand on her knee, and she'd swat it away. We'd have given her anything; she gave us nothing.

The one exception had been me, a month before. We'd been out on La Quebrada, all of us, out camping, with Marco and Julio passed out in the tent. The moon rippled on the water, and I'd come up behind Maria, confident with alcohol, and placed my arm around her. She'd laid her head upon my shoulder, and I didn't breathe at all. Mysteriously, she'd asked if I thought people would always be the same—that they could never change. Then she shivered, and she said that sometimes she wanted to walk into the ocean until the waters collected over her head, so she could see it swirl.

That must be beautiful. I went to kiss her, and she left. But I had gotten further than Marco or Julio ever had. And that meant something. It had to.

Marco said, "Well, I don't see any harm in taking him for a drink or two."

Maria smiled, and something dipped within me. My ancestors are the Spanish, and that spirit of adventure showed in me. And though I knew Maria's eyes were of the wild, the ancient, angry part of me still yearned to conquer her.

THAT NIGHT, A STORM HIT ACAPULCO, and rain lashed against the screens as Rafa the barman brought us drinks. Julio leaned against the rail, the slap of water in his face, and Marco was pushed back in his chair, next to Maria, whose long skirt kicked up with the wind. I sat off to the side, and across the table from me was the leathery, lean-faced American, who had accepted Marco's invitation readily. Up close, Driscoll seemed younger, with sinewy skin, and as he rambled he spun coins, and caught them just before they clattered to the wood. He was talking about (what else?) his diving—though in fairness we had asked. There were thirteen seconds between waves at high tide, he said, which based on gravity would give you three seconds, at the top of the cliffs, to determine whether each wave was, in fact, The One. They had different personalities, he said. One wave might kill you. Another wave, he claimed, might seem like it welcomed you home.

Candles flicked against our faces, thunder rang, and I hated myself for being drawn to this illusion. And when, in the middle of some ridiculous story, his brown eyes darted towards Maria, thin mouth smiling, I exclaimed, "Why do you even do it?"

Conversation ceased. They looked my way. I said, "It doesn't make a lot of sense. To me."

Driscoll said, "If I were to explain why, I would need far more time than this evening. It's not a pleasant story."

"Well, that's dramatic. My story is unpleasant too, but I'm not leaping off of cliffs."

Driscoll paused, and then said, "I jump because God tells me to."

The others nodded.

"What kind of answer is that?" I asked.

"The only one you'll understand."

"I see. Well, that's better than it could have been. I thought you came down for the women."

Driscoll turned away and then, at Marco's urging, we talked of other things: the storm, the damage it would do, and whether it would interfere with the road being constructed to Mexico City. This topic quickly fell apart, and Julio mentioned a shipwreck that he'd heard about, several hundred yards off the cliffs. It was preserved, he said, and you could dive down to the wreckage. Julio talked about swimming through the portholes to look for sunken treasure or Chinamen, since he'd heard it was a junk from years ago. How many years he didn't know, and so Marco asked Driscoll, who'd been here longer than any of us, when the ship had gone down. Driscoll couldn't recall. His hands were trembling. A moment later, Driscoll left, the screen door slamming behind him.

"I told you it was a bad idea," I said proudly.

I looked toward Maria, but her seat was empty, pushed out from the table. And the screen door slammed again.

ON AUGUST 23, I RETURN to Acapulco and visit Marco, who embraces me. He has remained here all these years. Marco works as a law clerk for a hotel rivaling the Miramar, which is constructed on the site where Driscoll dove, and where the divers leap today—at 7:00 a.m., and then again at 12:30 and 8:00. He tells me about his work, which involves copying legal contracts that keep amateur divers from suing the hotels. Then, when all our pleasant topics are exhausted, Marco tells me, quietly, that he was sorry to hear about my loss. I may stay as long as I like.

I am hit with the sudden image of Donna, an American woman I met in Mexico City, after I left Acapulco. Two vehicles careen towards one another, and her body crashes against a windshield, pushes through glass, skids against the pavement. Her face is almost gone. Then I am on Marco's couch again, graciously accepting his thoughts. Marco says he would have sent a card, but . . . and I tell him to stop. Marco is not the kind of friend you expect cards from.

He is, however, there when you need him.

Marco tells me I am I welcome to borrow his car and go exploring tomorrow, but he warns me that the place has changed. Acapulco has become so glitzy the palm trees are getting jealous. People do not come to see them anymore; they come to see the mosaic tile trees of Diego Rivera that line the hotels. They do not come to worship the oceans; they come to see the sculpted Virgin Mary placed beneath the water. I smile. I have heard about this Virgin in Mexico City, and I think to myself, for what feels like the thousandth time, that Driscoll—and Donna, as well—would have liked her very, very much.

MARCO IS RIGHT ABOUT THE CHANGES. In the newly paved plaza, the colonial trees shade tourists, who have come in droves to see the divers, buy the trinkets, and marvel at the glib fluidity of Nahuatl tongue. The once calm greens and whites have been replaced by blues, and reds, and sparkling yellows. And everywhere, like snapshots of celebrities, are portraits of the divers.

As I pass a market cart, I see a tin, mechanical display that pulls up tiny divers with a clicking, whirring sound, then tosses them off preformed cliffs before they make the climb again. Beside it, as though offended, squats a small stone carving of Quiahuitl, with a flimsy paper card. I pick it up, and read that Acapulco means "the place where reeds are broken." According to legend, the city was founded where a lovesick *Nahuatl* warrior, denied the object of his affections, wept until the tears turned his body into mud, and then reeds, his children, sprung out from his corpse. The God Quezalcoatl (furious with the girl's father) turned her into a cloud, and when this cloud floated over Santa Lucia the girl, this figure of Quihuitl, recognized the reeds as her lover's children and hurled herself upon them in rain, tearing them from their roots. Mud mingled with rainwater, and the lovers joined with nature. And Acapulco found its name.

I smile, and imagine myself retelling this story to Donna, her beaming back at me. It is an idealized memory, I know. While Donna smiled often, we were equally sad at times. I avoid the cliffs for now, and then find myself standing before city hall, where Maria's father worked for years. I spit on the ground. I remember a time when this building aroused rage in me, rage that even if I could convince Maria to love me (which I desperately, childishly needed to do) that love would be blocked by this man, a man who, despite his power and influence, did not comprehend the men his daughter knew, or her attempts to fill a void within her. I knew so little, though. I didn't know that Maria's father, in addition to being a businessman, was also a drunk. I didn't know that he would souse himself with tequila and linger in her doorway, then hit or touch her depending on his frustrations. I didn't know the older kids knew this, and that was why Maria hung around with us. And even though I understand, now, how foolish I was to love her, or to *believe* I loved her, at the time I just saw Driscoll stealing away a wild girl I knew I deserved, no matter what my poverty implied. I thought that she adored him for his mystery, his arrogance. But beyond this, I thought she cherished him because he alone, of all of us, had the courage to jump.

AFTER MARIA LEFT US THAT NIGHT at Rafa's, she began to spend more and more time with Driscoll, and I began to follow them, throughout the weeks, as she stayed with him while he played, admired him while he worked. I'd stalk them, watching at a distance, and he seemed to treat her tenderly. But Maria must have seen me. One day, as I sat shining shoes in the plaza, a pair of bare feet appeared before me, and I followed them up to the suntanned face of C. H. Driscoll.

He said we needed to talk.

We took a boat to La Roquetta Island, where the underbrush exploded into vibrant light and cool, reflective water. There were lovers in the cove, splashing themselves, but silence draped around us, and we felt alone. Driscoll said, "You once asked me why I jumped. Would you really like to know?"

I answered, "Yes."

"A few years ago, I was on a steamship bound from Portland to San Francisco, and the boiler room exploded, blasting a hole in the side. We sank in less than three minutes. Only ten people got to a raft. I was one of them."

Birds chirped, and the joyous lovers splashed. One of them dove off a rock and swam under water, emerging between the legs of the other one, propelling her into the air.

"I lost my wife," he said.

They'd been separated when the ship went down. She'd seen him in the raft, and started swimming, beating against the current, and he'd tried to paddle towards her. The other men restrained him, though, and her body sank into the Pacific, tugged down by the maw. She'd never screamed. Driscoll was unable to speak, and then continued, "I was on the raft for ninety-two hours." The sun had pounded them, while now and then one of the swarming gulls pulled in its wings and dove, pecking at the dead or slowly dying. Sharks circled the raft and bumped it, tried to flip it, so they pushed the dead men out. After seventy-five hours, only two of them remained alive, and they fought the seagulls more aggressively, catching one. They ate it raw. Seventeen hours later, a steamer from Hong Kong picked them up and ferried them to San Francisco. And there he stayed, with nothing to his name.

"What happened to the other man?" I asked.

"He killed himself. I almost did it too, but one of the crewmen told me about this place. He said he'd taken spice here, years ago. And so I went. After a year of waiting, staring at the cliffs, I knew that God had kept me alive for a reason, but I couldn't find it. I was lost. And so each year, on August twenty-seventh, I jump. I don't know, now, if I'm still trying to live, or just not trying very hard to die."

"So is that why you jump? To die?"

"I jump to prove God wants me here. It had to be a mistake, I felt. Some grand mistake. I jump to prove this wrong." Driscoll turned then, saying, "Listen to me. This is a story of miracles. That I got to the raft is a miracle. That I lived on the sea is a miracle. That the steamer found us, *that* is a miracle, and now . . . now another miracle has come. Jose, when I look at Maria she is the very image of my Lydia. They are the same."

"She isn't her." I pressured out, the statement like a bullet.

"I didn't say that they were. But they are the *same*. I believe it with all my heart." He looked at me, evaluating me. He turned away. "You'll understand it when you're older."

The sounds of lovers broke our silence. I remember wondering what hope there was for either of us—and while there may be none for him, I felt there might have been for me. But then, the following evening, I followed him and stood atop the cliffs, looking down into the ocean, towards the shoreline, and I saw him kiss her. I yelled, then, at the top of my lungs that night, and soon they turned to face me.

Watching them, I knew that if I jumped, if I could leap as he had done, she'd know, know that I loved her too. Maria screamed, and Driscoll charged the cliffs while I bent my knees and imagined the rush—the pummeling brace of the fall through the air—and I knew my time had come. And then, to my surprise and shame, my knees gave under me.

Each time I pushed they just gave more, and I felt my spirit collapsing. I knew I couldn't do it, knew that Driscoll could, and I realized, overwhelmingly, that I understood nothing.

Driscoll reached me.

"I can't do it." I said, shaking. "No. I can't."

Driscoll stared at me, amazed. In a rush, I saw him floating in the Pacific, fighting birds, watching his wife, and it was real to me. But when Driscoll reached to comfort me, my heart began to pound, my stomach twisting. I would not be beaten.

Maria, I was sure, was crashing up the cliffs towards us, but in that moment, night was dark. We were alone. Driscoll removed his arm and stood, his back to me. And as I rushed him from behind, he must have heard my heels against the dirt because he turned, and gasped as my shoulder collided with his chest. He staggered backward, and my fist connected with his jaw. It spun him around, and Driscoll was over the cliff before I understood what had happened, how close to the edge he was, how close I am. Then he was gone. The realization hit me slowly, swirling, and for the second time that night my knees give out from under me. The world went white, the ospreys wailed, and the ground rushed up to strike me in the face.

I WOKE ALONE, AND DIDN'T KNOW whether Maria reached the top. I still don't know. But the next day she was gone. Her father organized a search (which spread through Mexico) and with this other more significant disappearance, Driscoll went unnoticed. And when people acknowledged his absence, weeks later, they couldn't agree on how long he had been gone. Later, when Rigoberto Apac Rios began to jump the cliffs for money, only a few people even remembered Driscoll; everyone else just got into the show.

Everyone, that is, but me.

I stayed in Acapulco, in the plaza, until the dives began drawing tourists, and our little port city became famous and exotic. Then I fled. In Mexico City, and in Donna, I thought that I had finally found forgiveness. Instead, as I watched her pull away, leaving me standing on the steps to watch the accident, I only understood what Driscoll must have felt. What I did to Driscoll *was* an accident. I swear. And what happened to Donna, who gave me undeserved grace, was a mistake. It had to be. But only now, as I come back to Acapulco, broken, can I truly know for sure.

On August twenty-seventh, I step out into the morning sun. Then, while Marco sleeps, I approach the cliffs of *La Quebrada*. Sometimes, in these hours, I have seen lovers curl together on one of the Miramar's many balconies, their hearts and limbs entwined, but now I stand alone. I feel the solitude that Driscoll must have known, and then imagine Maria wading through the water, drifting out, then looking up to meet me. And then, as always happens in my evenings in the dark, when I wake with a cry as tragedies combine into a single, shapeless fear, her face morphs into Donna's, and the current tugs her away. And then it's time.

As the sea wind tears against me, pushing me back from the edge, I bend my knees. Donna's face has vanished into sunlight flecks, which dance upon the surface of Santa Lucia, and when I hurtle towards them, although I press with all the strength I still possess, I do not jump so much as fall, and it seems to happen slowly, like the ocean reaches toward me. Time pulses rhythmically. Each rock becomes a year, each wave (I think I see them all, it takes so long) a moment recollected. I try to arc my body now (the rocks swing closer), caught up in the swell to save some dignity. Halfway through the dive (has it been years now, where is youth?) I decide, victoriously, that my last moment will not be a graceless slap, like a stricken gull hitting the tide pools, and I align myself against the waves. The water is rushing up at me now, with rocks on the perimeter, and the cyclone has become a drain, which pulls me down to the just perfect spot, and suddenly (though even now I cannot say I saw it) I believe that I see Donna, on the rocks, her arms stretched out before I slit the water open. This vision, then, is lost in blackness as I feel the ocean grab me. Silence. The current flips me, light breaks darkness, and a small voice whispers "breathe" before I gasp air at the surface and am sucked back down again. This happens three more times. Then, finally, the back of my head collides with solid mass, and I release my air in a waterlogged scream before the warmth of Acapulco coats my skin, and the breeze is cool upon my flesh.

Another wave rights me.

I drift upon the beach, open my eyes, and see the fractured cliffs of La Quebrada towering fifty yards away. And then, as though awakening from sleep, I push myself upon the banks and start to weep, both suddenly and violently, awash and defiant of random tragedies, and stripped of all my youth, and cleansed.

DAPHNE'S COMPLAINT TO SRYINX SORINA HIGGINS

I fled in terror from the ravishing god
whose human beauty and divine desire
kindled his skin, inflamed his gaze,
and flushed my face with longing for his fire
to pour its molten power in secret places.
But I knew my body could not bear
his touch, and so I fled—immortal breath
behind my heels. His fingers singed my hair!
His golden arms reached out! I cried for Mercy:
Mercy, sweet and weary, heard: her weak
enchantment turned my naked limbs hard brown,
to hide from gods' eyes under fronds and leaves.
    You thought you had escaped the gods. And yet,
    They fashion poetry and music from our flesh.

SEMELE'S EXAMPLE SORINA HIGGINS

This love was tender, terrible: a sweet
self-sacrificing passion. As he kissed
her feet, he promised anything she wished
and swore upon the sacred river Styx.
No love had been like this: so strong it threw
his power down as plaything for her homely
hands—but she was different, for she only
asked to know him in his unveiled glory,
Only that! Zeus groaned and shuddered earth
with weeping, but his oath stood still. In pain
no god had known, he stripped off human raiment,
and, as he knew she must, she died in flames.
    Poor mortal fool. Yet would I be as brave
    Even if I knew my son-god would be saved?

WEDDING DAY SORINA HIGGINS

The red buds ripen on the waking trees
and tumble with the rain drops, leaving leaves
to tremble open, while they stain the mud
with empty husks like spattered springtime blood.
The yearly virgin earth has shed her sign
of purity before the god of time
who ravishes his bride with vernal love
when April's greening resurrection comes.
So every year, or day, would I be pure,
unfurling righteousness before my Lord.
But when He takes me to Himself, a stain
spreads foul and winter-smelling from my sin.
Instead of mine, my Bridegroom's blood appears:
His virtue and His crimson, spattered Springtime tears.

RELINQUISHED MARGOT STARBUCK HAUSMANN

THOUGH I HAD NEVER BEEN ONE to fall prey to the second deadly sin in its more socially sanctioned expressions, like coveting my friends' designer handbags or footwear, I did envy a family who were adding twin Haitian girls to their brood of six children. As an adoptive parent and also as one adopted as an infant myself, my heart thrilled for each of these who were about to become kin.

With dinner in the oven, I dropped into my office chair to check email. My own children were mesmerized by the television during the few peaceful minutes before my husband came home from work. After deleting spam, I clicked open my friend's most recent adoption update.

> We have been told that when we visit the girls in Haiti we will be able to meet the birth family and see where the girls grew up.

Until that moment I hadn't been aware of international adoptions in which any members of the extended family were involved. What a good gift for those girls, I mused. I fantasized that they would stay in touch over the years with a grandparent or distant aunt.

A vehement outcry from the living room sofa interrupted my reverie. After separating the offending child from the offended I fell back into my chair and continued scrolling down the message.

> Then when it is time for the girls to leave Haiti and join our family, we actually will have someone else escort them from Haiti to our home in Denver.

I was perplexed, wondering why the couple wouldn't make the trip once more to bring their daughters home. Did part of me envy her? The morning we were to leave our home in North Carolina for Southeast Asia to adopt our son, I had come completely undone. I'd wept uncontrollably in the shower as I prepared to leave my two older children, just two and four years old. The thought of them missing, wanting, needing me during the two-week absence was wrenching. As soap and tears fell to the floor, I had reminded myself that our new son would be blessed by our undivided attention during the traumatic transition from Southeast Asia to his new home and family in the United States. I continued to rationalize the unnatural separation—which felt strangely familiar—as the last suds rinsed down the drain. The journey was to be the most difficult experience of my life.

Staring blindly at the computer screen, I wondered why my friends would choose not to travel with their new daughters during such a precarious passage? My mind searched to fill the void. As if to address the large cartoon bubble question mark over my head, the email continued.

> *I hear that trip can be pretty tough with the moms saying goodbye to their children in front of you.*

The birthmothers? Saying goodbye? To their *children*? *In front of adoptive parents*? The world around me and the one within stopped spinning.

Just then my husband arrived home. The back door burst open, sucking babbling children into its wake. Though I longed to speak to him, it was clear that it could be hours before I would have uninterrupted access to him. The moment he set foot in the house he was pummeled by a dissonant trio of narratives describing the day's events.

In the midst of the domestic frenzy, I was frozen. Every neural pathway in my body jammed up as I attempted to process the information I'd read.

Deadened, I went through the rote motions of dinner, baths, and bedtime stories. We finally wrapped up the day with prayers for scraped knees, elderly relatives, and ailing stuffed animals. Once the children were settled, I returned to my study and to my friend's email. While my husband finished rinsing dinner dishes in the kitchen, I bellowed the words again for his fresh ears in hopes that doing so might make what seemed absurd more sensible.

"How could children with *parents* be adopted?" I demanded of him and of the world. "Nothing about that seems right. Orphans are adopted. Parents raise their children. End of story."

Wisely, my husband listened patiently to his bride's tirade while resisting the urge to offer sane comment.

Dishes continued to clink in the kitchen sink as my mind faded to screensaver mode. I made a mental list of authorities whom I deemed to be in a position to confirm or deny this atrocity. One was a well-known adoption advocate with connections to a number of leading figures in the national adoption community. Another was a local nurse missionary to Haiti. This woman had devoted herself to ministry with Haitian Christians and traveled there frequently. The third was an indigenous Haitian pastor widely respected in Haiti and abroad. Surely these would shed light on what seemed, to my mind, an incredibly unjust situation.

I felt certain that the fervent advocate would storm, "You're kidding! That's outrageous! We're going to let the world know that this is happening!" I could clearly picture her opening her laptop, while assuring me, "I'm posting it on the list-serve right now. We're going to get some action on this."

Surely if she knew of this situation the nurse missionary, with a single tear rolling down her cheek would choke out, "That's horrible. I have never heard of such a thing." She would be visibly touched by the suffering of the people she loved. With her compassionate heart for the Haitians, I imagined her reasoning, "If it happens, it must be rare." Her face, in my mind's eye, bore the agony these families had endured.

The final champion to make an appearance in my vision was the wise pastor. With solemn countenance, I could almost hear him confirming in a thick Haitian accent, "Yes, it is true. Our people are so very poor. Parents see this as a way for their children to survive. It is very sad indeed." He would continue to describe his church's work among the poor, "We provide support for these families, but many are simply devastated by poverty. They see the orphanages as their only option."

The kitchen was now silent and dark. Though I heard my husband in our bedroom, settling in for the night, I continued perusing the lengthy email. I scrolled through the requisite account, which attempted to explain the incomprehensible.

> *I guess in Haiti the moms are so desperate for someone to care for and feed their kids that they are thankful to get the children into an orphanage and it becomes quite the competing business for who has the best orphanage, etcetera. The moms are then still able to visit the children . . .*

Enough. I tottered off toward bed now sensing a new distance from my friend. The magical thread knitting us together as adoptive parents had too quickly unraveled. Was I crazy? Would others react to the formation of her family as strongly as I?

I knew they wouldn't. As I glanced in the doorway at my sleeping children, I was reminded of the largely homogenous response we'd received from our family and friends after adopting from a country struggling to care for its children. Blind to a child's unfathomable loss the well-meaning would say, "Bless you. It's such a good thing you've done. Your reward is in heaven." Like me, my friend would politely deny it, yet some of the warmth would linger.

Still unsettled, I climbed under the covers.

I had no reason to question the integrity of these friends. Fluffing my pillow, I tried to convince myself that it was all for the best. Thoughts of terrified children being ripped from maternal arms and shipped to what in their experience was akin to another planet nagged at me. I wanted to believe that under such grave circumstances all this could, somehow, be warranted. I tried to rationalize the seismic emotional and cultural rupture endured by these older children as legitimate. At last I nodded off with my mind still scanning for resolution, now furiously spinning to resolve the conundrum which so suddenly and forcefully demanded my attention and energy.

THE BEDSIDE CLOCK GLOWED 2:37 A.M.

With the clarity that only middle-of-the-night awakenings afford, I realized that my indignation had been projected onto unwitting pale-skinned and dark-skinned players. In that strangely lucid moment it became clear that my angst was not only about them.

I, too, had been relinquished while my own parents had been living. The few brief paragraphs my adoptive family had received on crisp adoption agency letterhead, noting the height, ethnicity, hair and eye colors of my biological parents, had failed to make them seem real. Essentially, they had been dead to me.

My choice of "expert witnesses"—advocate, nurse, and pastor—voiced the rage, confusion, and sadness, which were in fact my own. The adult child curled beneath my covers had lived too long under the blanket of an unconscious fear. For too long I had quelled the expression of my authentic anger, doubt, and grief. In my deepest places I was—understandably, I think—unsure that those around me could tolerate my truest self.

Those three witnesses bore such striking resemblance to another trinity of authoritative friends at my disposal. The first is the fiery one who advocates on my behalf. The next is the human one, who hurts for the hurt of his people. Finally, I saw the face of the paternal one who longs for justice to reign on earth as it is in heaven.

The three I had invoked to judge my friend became, after all, the One I myself needed.

KNOWING TOO MUCH TRISTA SWING

What a disappointment—
the mind of God
opened like the back
of a doll house.

Mysteries laid out like tiny
porcelain dolls.
Pluck an answer out,
a tiny body removed from its stiff bed
under a kleenex blanket.

What an ugly gift
I have asked for.

Watch it walk to the table.
No. Watch the large hand
which walks it. Fingerprints
a vortex of centipedes
pressing into the plastic waist.

He drags her legs, dead sticks,
across the floor
in His desired direction
toward a man

who wears a tiny tie,
and has a plastic head.
They kiss. It's dry,
like the tips of apple
stems touching. Neither likes
it, nor dislikes it.

PARENTS TRISTA SWING

She struggles to sit up, to escape
the honey stain of afterbirth,
and plays with her belly
like an empty balloon.

The baby, like a doll,
rests on her arm.
If she had his number
she'd call the father,
tell him she's got proof of love.

Love led them, after all,
fumbling in the ash night,
stumbling to the back
of the El Camino, feeling
each others' soft bodies
like baby blankets.
Love left the truck bed
tracks on her back.

Beside her bed
the next lover shifts
from one foot to the other,
passing her a Tonka truck.
She reaches out and takes his hand.
The smell of iron from her blood
clings to the air.

He tells her he will stay up with it at night.
She smiles and drives the truck across her legs.

THE HEALER JUDY LEE GREEN

In a cooler
he carried
his lifeless baby
down the aisle
through music,
songs, shouts,
prayer, applause,
to the healer
who claimed to have raised
the dead.

He lifted the lid,
placed on the altar
her cold stiff body,
fell to his knees,
arms stretched heavenward.
Tears flooded his eyes,
washed down his face.

Jesus! The healer prayed
above chords of "Amazing Grace."
*Give her life! Give
this baby life. Give
this little girl life. We
plead with you, Lord!*

*You raised Lazarus
from the dead in John 11.
You raised the twelve-year-old daughter
of Jairus from the dead in Matthew 9,*

THE HEALER

*Mark 5 and Luke 8. You returned to life
a widow's son from his coffin
in Luke 7. Lord, we believe in miracles.
We believe in your Son. We believe
in the Holy Spirit.
Give her life!*

Thousands of spectators
in the auditorium prayed,
shouted, wept openly,
were struck by the Holy Ghost,
spoke in tongues, danced
in aisles, bounced up and down,
swayed to and fro, waved arms,
collapsed flat on the floor.

The healer softly touched,
gently nudged, then shook
the precious doll. Hours later,
defeated, heart-broken,
the anguished father
tenderly returned
the empty corpse
to the picnic cooler
and closed the lid.

A REED SHAKEN IN THE WILDERNESS DEVIN O'DONNELL

Then the Sabbath came. This night when all other nights bowed their heads, when all feelings refined their metaphysics into a molten heat, and when all forms of shame and insecurity and redundancy were distilled into one great, unencumbered release: the Night Service at The Horn of Michael's Gospel Church.

David had put on his casual attire and his wife wore hers. He took pleasure in his flip-flops; he reveled in his Polarfleece, and today his neck was not choked with a tie. He longed for this night, thirsted for it in his cottonmouth soul. This last week came and went like every other week. A week of wishing he worked somewhere else, then of estrangement from his family because he had to provide for them, then of self-pity, then of a wife who doesn't look like the visions in his office, then of a disobedient son, then of doing what he does not want to do, then of nothingness, and then of Jean Fridays at the office. All this gave birth to new lines and wrinkles in his features, the entire workweek creeping silently into his lackluster face as he bore it all with stoical effort. He was civic, if not boring, if not dead, at times dragging himself through the hot turbulence of day and the cold machinery of night. He would occasionally pick up his children from school, drive home and not say a word to them, the radio going the entire time with the pulsed cadence of NPR. Another day he might leave the office early and kill the afternoon looking for houses and cars he could not buy. Another day he might put in five hours of ergonomic overtime, poised neatly in his chair, in solidarity, in the evening, his office lit up with the artificial glow of computer-haze. But every week it seemed as though he'd waited all his life for this night.

He was driving now, casually and unhurried, lightly bobbing his head to the music. He was unknotting himself in preparation for the evening. He thought of the music that was coming and of the Spirit coming with it, borne on the clouds of a forte-swelling chorus, the mighty dithyramb of Jericho leveling the heart and mind. This evening, however, he was more excited than usual. He had done something extraordinary, an act that actually made these last days tolerable. A week ago he invited a friend to the Night Service. She now sat quietly in the back seat of the Dodge Caravan, he and his wife in the front. The blonde-haired woman was an acquaintance in the Neighborhood Alliance, a single mother equally concerned for protection and safety. Her name was Michelle, and he would see her at the weekly meetings, noting the pathos behind her suggestions of increased security and motion-detecting floodlights. David could not recall how long ago he had begun to feel strangely toward her. It was a feeling he could not completely identify, a feeling he did not want to know truly, even if he could: something between pity and fondness, a half-trusted feeling. Her vulnerability and plight as a single parent combined with the shape of her face and figure glinted in the light of his affection. And perhaps it was not complicated at all, perhaps it was as simple as the fact that when he spoke to her, she smiled. It was the kind of smile that held bright promises in it, the likes of which he had not seen on the face of wife for some time. For this reason, this simple smile, David asked Michelle to attend his church. But as he now glanced in his rear-view mirror, David could see no such smile play on her lips. She gazed out the window, her face innocent and vacant in expression. He knew she had never been to the Night Service before, but as they drove up to the place of worship David felt in his somewhat anxious heart that he had done the right thing.

It was a square building, large and simple, with multiple entrances on its three sides. They entered beneath a sign that read, "Welcome to The Horn of Michael's Gospel Church." The foyer wrapped around in a circle with each inner entrance leading into the worship center, a large and open hall with seats descending. Perhaps Michelle felt obliged to sit in the rear because it was darker, but the truth was that there were never any seats up front near the stage. The room was half-lit, relinquishing a messy glare to the paintings hanging from the ceiling.

"This is an experiential church," David said as they stood in the aisle. He was not looking at his wife.

"Oh," said Michelle. She looked around, seeming half-disturbed by the setting. Watching her, David noticed it too, suddenly aware of the strangeness in the paintings that surrounded them: a man with sheep, the same man putting his hands on people, the same man, again, surrounded by children with the words "Forbid Them Not" beneath it. He listened too, now keenly aware of the crowds of people speaking a bright and barbaric language, with hopeful faces and gestures full of future tenses.

As they took their seats in the back of the sanctuary, David leaned over to Michelle. "Here comes the worship team."

Just then, a mixed group of men and women took position on the stage. The songs began softly. The light became almost completely swallowed by the dark, except for the stage, and the empty spaces in the room filled with a growing concentration of bodies. The herd-like multitude now subsumed a grey mass in the front, now becoming one body of many dark heads and arms and feet. As the music progressed, diffusing into the empty spaces of the sanctuary, Michelle remained seated though David and his wife stood with the rest of the congregation, hands in the air. As was his custom, he wanted to go forward, but he remained standing beside Michelle in the rear of the room. He didn't blame her for not standing. She might not be sincere, he thought; there is nothing worse than doing things simply because everyone else is doing them. His wife left him, drawn to the front and into the stirring, scattered congregation. "Sometimes," David said, turning toward Michelle, "It feels good to just breathe His presence."

"Whose?" Michelle blinked.

David stammered, looking straight ahead.

"His." He was pointing up in the air, his face serious.

Pushing away all other sound, the music worked its way further into all things, pressing into the bones. David's eyes were closed, hands stretching to the infinite, feet tapping the rhythm. The songs went on, choruses ringing out in ecstatic release. They shouted things and called out to the Spirit. With every new song David was unshackled. Like a rock into a still pond, it stirred the mud-bottom of his heart. A cold sheen glossed his forehead. He wiped his face and put his hand back in the air. His bland and rounded countenance became pointed and sharp with furrowed emotion, and then his face shifted into intense delight. But he caught himself, opening his eyes to see Michelle immediately turn away, as if she was somewhat ashamed for looking at him in this manner.

David's eyes were still closed when the musicians stopped playing, put down their instruments, and one by one exited the stage. The room was still. He opened his eyes, as if coming back from a long way off. The elongated silence told everyone it was time to sit down. David was relieved.

Then the preacher received his pulpit, a middle-aged man slightly overweight mounting the stairs in front. He wore black Levi's, his belly impinging upon his small legs in trivial protrusion over his belt, his unbuttoned white shirt revealing the skin of his neck and chest. He opened his mouth, his words coming in cadenced pauses and clipped sentences, rising and falling in volume. His brow wrinkled tight with each supplication.

"Heavenly Father—You—are God. We just want to praise *You*—this even-ing. We thank You—that we have been—baptized in the Spirit—that we can—speak the tongues of heaven—that we can—see the power of Your hand. We ask You now—to give—Your Holy Spirit in liberality and in might—that You would—*glorify!*—Yourself. In the name of Jesus—and Amen."

Michelle sat motionless and expressionless, closed mouth and wide-eyed. David watched his wife coming back to him in her heavy gait, head down and alone, her hips moving out of sync with her arms. She wore jeans and a loose-fitting shirt, modest and unnoticeable, her brown and course hair reaching the length of her shoulders as it had for five years. At that moment as in others, he did not want to be married to her. She glanced at him, unsmiling. Looking beyond her, he focused now more intently on the preacher.

"The question I want to ask you this evening—has to do with God's power. Beloved, do you believe in God's power?"

A volley of yeses and amens went forth.

"Yes, but do you *believe*," his voice falling now, "in God's *power*? I dare say you do, but there are some in this congregation—some among us now—who do not. Some of you have not seen his *power*. And to you I am speaking now. The Lord shakes the world. The mountains—tremble at his word. I want to suggest to those of you who cannot possibly know what I mean—that it is a good thing for the Lord to *shake* us now and then—Amen?"

The crowd answered in kind.

"Amen!" cried David. He ignored his wife's look of surprise. Though he rarely spoke out this early in the service, he felt it was good for Michelle to see him like this, undignified, uninhibited in the Spirit, ready to dance naked before her eyes and all eyes.

"In the eleventh chapter of Matthew's gospel, Jesus asks the people the same question—for what did you go out in the wilderness to see, a reed shaken by the wind? Is that why you are here—tonight? To see a reed shaken in the wilderness? If that's what you think about the power of God, you will see greater things than that—hallelujah! This night we came to see the power of God—and like Jacob we will not let him go unless he blesses us—Amen?"

"Amen!" The people roared.

Closing his eyes, the preacher grew quiet suddenly, and invoked the concentration of his listeners in a low and subdued voice.

"Heavenly Father—I ask—that—that—You would *shake* us this even-ing—that You would—show Your power in the wilderness for us all to see and feel. Jesus, glorify Yourself now—by sending out Your Spirit upon us—in Your holy name—Amen."

The congregation sounded forth in robust approval, and the preacher descended the steps but did not go back to his seat. He stood in the front as the musicians took the stage again. The lights dimmed. The leader, a short man standing in front of a keyboard, spoke in a soothing voice.

"I know many are hurting and are lost. Many need healing, many need forgiveness. Come forward now. Cry out to Him now. Now is the time. Feel the release only He can give. He will set you free. He is moving. Sing to God now and allow His Holy Spirit to shake you."

David smiled and stood up. Michelle sat still. David's wife left him again, moving toward the front where the crowd re-gathered, assimilating the denseness of bodies. The music started with whole notes, sustained, elongated, suspended in the air. A woman's voice began in soft incantation.

"Did you feel the mountains tremble? Did you hear the ocean's roar?"

Just beneath it, drums faintly throbbed and ushered in the tempo, moving and building in volume until suddenly a surge of voices rose into chorus. The onlookers gathered against the front of the stage, haphazardly forming a line. The preacher shouted, moving down the line of people. One by one, he paused and placed his left hand on their shoulder and his right hand on their forehead.

David, impetuous and brash, squeezed Michelle's hand. He smiled at her surprised look and pulled her toward the front, through the crowd, placing her next to him in the line with the others. She did not fight against him. He told himself later that she had followed willingly.

"You will see, Michelle," David shouted, the music loud and thundering.

She tried to speak.

"Don't be afraid," David said. "Just be willing." He began praying softly, almost inaudibly.

As the preacher moved down the line, the music moved on, without crescendo or climax, building in din and clamor, in beautiful dissonance, building too in heat and in love. David looked up at the singers, suddenly struck by their appearance, noting their sweated face, radiant and fatigued, with a spray of yellow light glistening on their skin. He was seeing things he had not seen before, but he put the strangeness of it behind him. The preacher moved closer. Every person he touched, David's wife among them, broke out into frenzy, grown men and women uncontrolling themselves, leaping and whirling before the ark, their bodies shaking in fits of praise and chaos. The preacher then turned to see David. Still holding her hand, he seemed to present Michelle to the man. The preacher's face flashed with delight, and he nodded assuring them. He placed his hands on both their foreheads and began repeating, "Holy Spirit come, Holy Spirit come, come Holy Spirit."

David began to tremble as the minister said these words. His tremble grew to full shaking, and he soon dropped, flailing happily against the floor, his face in the shadows, the dewy wisps of hair plastered to his brow with sweat. And even here he could not help from desiring to peer out at her from his trembling sacrament and find in that one glimpse some smiling approval in her countenance. But he saw disdain written on her face—she despised him in her heart.

The music kept on, the tempo now pumping blood to the heads of many. The preacher put his other hand on Michelle's shoulder in a concentrated movement, again repeating,

"Come Holy Spirit, come," louder each time until he was yelling, red-faced, with eyes burning. She stood unmoved with a mystified expression. Once more the preacher yelled, "Holy Spirit, come!" David watched as the preacher thrust her head back in whiplash. Her body followed and she fell, striking her head on the floor in a sound like bruising of an apple. Her eyes rolled to the back of her head. The music began to fade. David had never seen this kind of shaking before, violence in her limbs and joints, a kind of obscene epilepsy taking over. He looked at the preacher, whose mouth was open and moving. When his words finally came, they were frantic and strained. He knelt down beside her, placing his hand on her shaking forehead and began to repeat, "O God, O God, O God, Come Holy Spirit, come. Have mercy on us."

David could not tell if she was dying. At first there was nothing, only the sound of faith cracking in half. Then the fit subsided. Michelle rolled to one side and lay still, eyes closed and calm, her chest expanding and contracting with each involuntary breath. The preacher began breathing with her, heavily and instinctively. People stood gathered around, their faces blank, draining of color, afraid and bewildered. Looking on, David suddenly felt the need to be near his wife. He turned away and found her in the crowd. He took her hand, trembling gently. The preacher looked up to heaven.

"We have seen your power—O God. You have indeed—shown us mercy. We have seen—a great sign today. God has shaken this dear woman from darkness into light, from death into life everlasting."

And while the multitude marveled, David hid his face in his hands and wept.

THE READING KELLY BELMONTE

The card is dealt:
In a poorly lit room, the reader thumbs
a well-worn deck, pulls
a pale and perfect beauty
with eyes of steel
and a mouth like Mona Lisa.
The reader intakes a just audible gasp,
and I smell the fear, the expectation
of dozens of pale, balding men
and dark, foreign women
entering these doors before me,
one at a time,
all waiting.

"What does this mean?" I ask.
A pause, a drag from her cigarette,
she glances
at me, then away.

I wait as those who came before me
waited—like women in early labor,
like illegal immigrants,
like twilight—for hope
to be held out to them,
for a glimpse of control,
a certainty of what they suspected:
mortality.

Another drag, the reader begins:
"Hands bound in front,

THE READING

she sees her restraints
and this:
her captor left a way out.
She refuses.
She stays in that stance,
smiling, coldly knowing
in her bondage,
she maintains control."

A slow cloud of blue smoke
as the reader exhales, a glimpse
brushing my eyelid,
and then, almost too casually,
"You tell me."

TORN VEIL LISA OHLEN HARRIS

"Carry them with you," Miriam whispered.

We slipped our shoes off inside the entryway, where a jumble of plastic sandals lay on the ground. In the open courtyard, pigeons clustered with light rustling of wings, so that even the creatures seemed to hush in reverence.

Miriam helped me arrange the black robe over my shoulders and head. I'd worn a scarf but hadn't thought to wear long sleeves, so the attendant loaned me a wad of fabric that unfolded into a hooded robe. Every other woman visiting the mosque that day wore her own street clothes, and though I tried to blend in, I always somehow missed Islamic propriety by an inch of sleeve or the slip of a scarf. The borrowed robe singled me out as the foreigner, the outsider. Instead of covering and equalizing, the black fabric exposed me. I was not a Muslim.

In bare feet, we followed the cold tile corridor to the shrine room, where it is said that the martyr's bones lie in a stainless steel tomb. The metal tomb was the only furnishing in that vast room. It sat like a throne in the great hall where icy white and blue tiles covered the many arches, walls, and supporting pillars. Chandeliers hung from the high domed ceiling. Steel grillwork made up four sides of the tomb, and a lone worshiper stood next to it, a woman wearing an embroidered robe like one of Aaron's priests, her lips moving in silent supplication. Instead of the Ark of the Covenant, she tended a casket. When she reached out to touch its holiness, she did not die.

Loneliness filled the great room and overflowed to blanket the courtyard beneath the open sky, loneliness so heavy it should have split the tiles, broken open the dome. But the structure held.

We settled on the floor a few meters back from the shrine. Miriam placed the soles of her shoes together so they wouldn't touch holy ground, and she tucked them under the fabric of my robe. Across the room, a man knelt with his arms wrapped around himself, bowing. Above him a chandelier glittered like a thousand icicles—a thousand and one tiny Damocles' swords.

The day's research topic was firm in my mind—marriage between Sunni and Shiite—but I couldn't remember specific questions from the memo pad I carried in my purse. My class leader had only consented to a day trip with a single informant because Miriam was Shiite, and we had very few Shiite contacts.

The woman at the tomb swayed, her face wet. She held a piece of cloth to her breast, white and clean against her dark clothing. With the cloth in her right hand, she leaned against the tomb, kissing the metal grille again and again.

"Why does she do that?" I asked.

"She wants a blessing," Miriam said. "But what she kisses is only silver."

I pulled out my memo pad to write *blessing* and *only silver*; I flipped pages of field notes to where I'd jotted down research questions based on the previous day's class meeting. Miriam dabbed her nose and eyes with a tissue.

"Today, no questions," she said. "No research. Today is for Saida Zainab."

I closed the memo pad—but I would get my notes somehow. The woman at the tomb kissed and polished with silent tears, seeking a blessing. The man under the chandelier bent so far forward that his forehead rested on the ground. Silence filled the mosque and overflowed to the courtyard.

Saida Zainab's shrine walls held tile after tile, the design of every square repeating the one next to it in a silent echo, lonely and lovely.

I THINK MOST OF THE PROPHETS WERE KILLED.
—Miriam, Shiite university student

The woman weeping at the shrine pushed one corner of the cloth through the grille surrounding the tomb. She tried to weave the fabric in and out, but the partition's metalwork grating was too tight.

"She thinks there will be a special power from Saida Zainab in the cloth," Miriam said. "Her life has been hard."

Shiites trace their religious heritage through lines of hardship and suffering back to Ali, the prophet Mohammed's cousin and son-in-law. Since Mohammed had no sons and Ali did, it was Ali who carried on the bloodline of the prophet's family and leadership of the new religion—according to Shiites. The Sunni branch rejected Ali and followed another line of leaders. So already in the second generation, the family of Islam was divided. Lady Zainab was Ali's daughter: like her father, she was assassinated; like her father, Zainab was a martyr.

"She suffered so much," Miriam said. "Our own hardships seem small compared to Saida Zainab's."

I'd read about the self-flagellation on the Day of Ashura and how faithful Shiites slash at themselves with whips and knives as a bloody reminder that blood ties them to Islam. Ali was the rightful successor to Mohammed, yet he suffered and died. Shiites revere suffering. By what conviction do they call down that suffering by cutting and whipping themselves? My own religion is built on a bloody foundation and on suffering, but I have yet to rend my own flesh.

"Through suffering, we remember," Miriam said.

I waited to hear what her suffering was, what she remembered. I was ready to memorize what she said, to excuse myself to wash hands in the fountain or get a breath of fresh air in the courtyard so I could write some quick research notes. Miriam gave me nothing but silence.

With no new notes coming from my time with Miriam, I would be assigned to seek out a different informant in coming days. If I kept getting key information from my friend, I could continue to count her as an informant and spend a few hours a week with her.

A stray pigeon flew low over the shrine and into the corners of the large room, desperate for a way out. It flapped and flew, as if drunk on loneliness, until it found the wide door. The pigeon landed in the courtyard near a woman and three children seated on the cold tile. The woman untied a piece of cloth, passing bread and boiled eggs to her children.

"They have no other place," Miriam said. "The poor come to Saida Zainab to rest." She spoke as if the martyr were living still. "They are hungry," Miriam said. "Let them eat."

But they would be hungry again.

WOULD YOU MARRY A MAN WHO WASN'T FROM DAMASCUS?
ARRANGED MARRIAGE? MARRY FOR LOVE?
—Ethnographic research questions

I met Miriam for the first time at Damascus University, where she was an English major. That first day, leaning against the wall outside a lecture hall, another student told me about a village outside of Damascus. Miriam stood close but didn't speak, even when the other student introduced her as a true Damascene whose grandfather's grandfather had been born there. But when the classmate mentioned that Miriam was not Sunni but

Shiite, I felt a rush of excitement and turned my questions to Miriam, Shiite university student.

She gave me short answers—yes, no, not sure—and looked past me, as if waiting for someone else. Even if she didn't like me, didn't want to talk with me, I was determined to interview this Shiite student, Miriam. I would be the first in my class to bring home field notes from an English-speaking Shiite contact.

In English only a few letters differentiate between Sunni and Shiite, but for the Muslim there is a world of difference. Presbyterian and Pentecostal understand this. Astronomer and Astrologer do, too. From the outside we see Christian, stargazer, Muslim. From the inside, a galaxy separates Sunni from Shiite.

Several days later I saw Miriam at the bus station near the university, where we found ourselves waiting for the same bus home. I told her where I lived, with a Syrian Orthodox family in the Old City. "I live not far from you," Miriam said. "Outside the Christian Quarter, nearer the Turkish bath."

My classmates would be impressed. Hidden right under our noses, a pocket of Shiites lived behind the doors we walked past nearly every day. Questions formed and clicked. How many? Do they intermarry? Is there a Shiite mosque nearby?

"Maybe I can visit your home sometime, Miriam. Are your neighbors all Shiite, too?"

She narrowed her eyes. Until now my Arab informants had invited me to their homes with no prompting, even upon our first introduction. Perhaps Shiites were more distant, self-protective. But Miriam was an Arab, and the pre-Islamic hospitality of her ancestors took over: she welcomed the wayfarer.

"You may come home with me now, today. Meet my mother and sisters."

Miriam lived in the Old City, just five minutes through stone corridors from my own host family. Her doorway looked exactly like every doorway surrounding it, the entry off the street so ancient, so low that we had to duck to enter.

Three years after I said goodbye to Miriam and left Syria, I returned to Damascus. My letters to Miriam had been returned as undeliverable, whether addressed in Arabic or in English. I hoped her family was still there in the Old City. I hoped that Miriam would remember me. But after three years' absence, the identical doors set in the stone walls of her lane confused me. I stood under an archway, unsure which door to try first.

An old man selling Pepsi at the corner left his cart and came to the archway. He gestured for me to follow and led me without hesitation. He knocked hard on a door, calling out that she was here—the girl from America had returned.

I didn't remember this old man, but he knew who I was and recognized me, even after three years' absence. I felt a sharp ache for my months in Damascus; I wished I'd paid more attention, learned more Arabic. I longed to go back and start over, to remain in Damascus, build a life there. The old man slipped back to his cart when Miriam's mother opened the door and gathered me in her arms with joyful tears of reunion.

Shiites always remember.

But on my visit to Miriam's home that first day, her mother hurried to greet me with a warm smile and a large mole on her upper lip. Months later, when I left Damascus, this ugly woman would capture me in an embrace while Miriam translated the words that reminded me of a Flannery O'Connor short story I'd read sophomore year.

"You are my daughter. You are my own child."

Miriam kept her head covered the day she introduced me to her family, though her mother and sisters were unveiled before me. She served me tea but didn't drink. I felt from her a reserve, a distance. Perhaps Miriam would never be a cooperative informant.

Her father joined us for the meal. He greeted me and gestured to where I should sit, between Miriam and her mother. So we sat and ate together, as I had with so many Arab families during my months in Damascus. A good Arab hostess, Miriam scooped more rice and vegetables onto my plate, refilled my drink each time I got it down to the halfway point. But she did not eat.

When the meal ended, Miriam's two sisters cleared the dishes and rolled up the mat. Her father leaned back against a bolster, and Miriam brought him a cigarette and matches.

With my memo pad and a short pencil in hand, I asked Miriam if she would translate for me. She made eye contact with her father, but he ignored her and looked to me kindly. Miriam chewed her bottom lip a moment before telling me to go ahead with my questions.

He prayed at the Shiite mosque near the Street Called Straight, he told me. He liked to visit the nearby Ommayed Mosque where the great martyr John the Baptist's head was enshrined. But the martyr he loved most was the Prophet's granddaughter Zainab, and as an expression of his devotion, he owned a small summer home near her shrine, on the outskirts of Damascus.

When I saw Miriam again, she smiled at me with her mother's warm smile. As we walked through campus, she linked her arm in mine. We found a splintery wooden bench and sat together while students rushed past us, most turning to gape at the foreigner. Miriam looked right at me as she spoke. She promised to teach me many things, to help me with my research, she said. Her father wanted me to know that I was welcome in his home every day, as one of his own children.

Miriam became my closest friend in Damascus. She eventually told me that her early distance was because she feared that I was a spy. Syrians, it seems, half expect any American they meet to be an undercover CIA operative. The memo pad and questions made Miriam suspicious and frightened. But her father laughed at her fears and was happy to answer my questions. Was your wife from Damascus? Are all of your family friends Damascenes? Would you let your daughters make friends with a Palestinian girl? With a villager? These, he told Miriam, were not the sorts of questions that a spy would ask. A spy would likely keep her memo pad hidden. A spy would be more clever than you, daughter. You would never suspect her. This one is not a spy. She is your friend.

IN PARADISE WE WILL DRINK FROM CUPS OF GOLD. WE'LL HAVE BETTER CLOTHES THAN WE EVER HAD HERE. I HOPE TO SEE YOU IN HEAVEN WITH ME, AND NOT IN HELL. INSHALLAH, I WILL BE THERE.
—Miriam, Shiite university student

I handed the black robe back to the attendant and slipped on my shoes. Her parents were already in the small house a few minutes' walk from the mosque, Miriam said. Her mother had carried in minced lamb for kabob; we would have a small holiday. An Arab lunch would stretch out my afternoon, and still I had no answers to my research questions for Miriam. It wasn't right for me to stay and socialize when I hadn't finished my ethnographic work for the day.

In a few hours, my classmates would all gather to compare and discuss their field notes. There was time for me to do a couple of interviews once I got back to Damascus, if I caught a bus back right away. I'd need to say hello to Miriam's parents and then return to Damascus and contact new informants to make up for my wasted morning. I would redeem the day.

"Just come," Miriam said.

We walked into the courtyard, and the fragrance of roasted meat rose to welcome us. Miriam's mother stepped around the fountain to greet me with a kiss, "Welcome, my daughters. You must eat." I was an ancient desert traveler, thirsty and hungry, in need of shelter. My hosts had killed the fattened calf.

The meal was set up on the ground beside the courtyard fountain. Miriam's father turned a spigot and a single stream of water rose, splashing as a late summer rain in the desert plops and spatters over the desperate parched earth. I wouldn't have to stay for long, but I could at least take time for the ones who called me daughter.

We ate meat and herbs with our fingers, on plates of bread. Miriam took up the aluminum water pitcher, pouring into the glass an echo of the sprinkling fountain behind us. Her mother knelt beside me and tore a piece of bread, ripped off a sprig of the fresh herb, and reached for the meat piled on a large round of bread before us. "Good health," she said, handing me the wrap of bread, meat, and herbs.

Miriam's father echoed the blessing, "Good health." And so they ministered to the stranger and sojourner, feeding me as one of their own. We ate together from that common loaf, all tearing hunks of bread and reaching for the meat and herbs.

Miriam poured water into the glass we would share. She held it out so I could drink first then refilled it and drank after me. After the meal, Miriam's mother and father retreated to one of the rooms that opened to the courtyard. Her father came out only to pull an extra mat into the other room for us.

"And now we will rest," said Miriam.

I imagined my classmates walking through hot streets in Damascus, finding informants, taking notes. I had nothing to show for my day, nothing to type up on a laptop that evening when the rest of my class would scurry to claim a computer and organize their notes into research topics. I would return from Saida Zainab empty-handed.

But my Shiite hosts had filled me, and I was sleepy. To honor them, I must rest. Research questions written across my closed eyelids stretched and drifted to the sound of the rain. Not rain—it was the fountain, baptizing the tiles, washing away the sand and dust. The sound filled the open courtyard and overflowed into the room where we rested, Miriam on one mat and I on another. It washed away my questions and thoughts of bus schedules back to Damascus. It lifted me to the place of trust and sleep.

MIRIAM SHOOK ME AWAKE. "Come with me."

Disoriented from the nap, I followed her out into the courtyard, where she handed me a thick cloth, her face as solemn as a priest's. She showed me how to fold the cloth over the handle of a steaming teapot so I could lift it without burning myself. Miriam took up a scratched aluminum tray with two small, clear glasses and a bowl of sugar. A scarf was drawn over her head loosely, with the ends untied and hanging from her temples like the long prayer curls I'd seen on Jewish worshipers.

We formed a two-woman procession across the courtyard, past the fountain where streams of water still flowed and splashed, sprinkling us as we passed. The drops made her face shine in the sunlight as she balanced the tray on her right hand to take hold of the wooden ladder that led to the roof. I climbed the wooden ladder after her, the teapot swinging in my hand, steam rising from it as if from a golden censer.

Once we had ascended to the rooftop, Miriam set the tray on a small platform made of several tile blocks stacked together. I set the hot teapot directly on the stone table, and we removed our shoes.

Overhead, the sky formed a blue dome, with the sun as its warm and brilliant chandelier. A breeze lifted my hair and teased at Miriam's loose scarf until she let it fall from her head. There were no men on surrounding rooftops to see the private glory of her hair.

Miriam confessed her secrets to me that afternoon, things she hadn't told anyone, not even her mother. There was a man, she told me, a gentle man. "Not a cousin, but he is good. If God wills, he will talk to my father. If God wills, he will come for me."

And she told me of growing up in Damascus and attending an Islamic school for girls, where a classmate became her best friend. She was like a sister, the friend Miriam had hoped and waited for. Miriam told her friend a family secret and found relief in sharing the burden of it—until she came home one afternoon to find her mother beating carpets and crying, her face dirty and wretched.

"We must not trust them, my daughter. The scorpion hides in walls and on rooftops. If you do not look around before you step, she will bite you."

There in Damascus, the city of their birth, their language, their religion—surrounded by households long established alongside their own—Miriam's family was alone. So they smiled at neighbors when they passed them on the lane, but they did not reach out in friendship. It is foolish to befriend a scorpion or a neighbor. Not one could be trusted.

"Even my brother's wife is not one of us," Miriam said. "A good friend would be trustworthy and true. I long for such a friend."

Miriam took up the teapot and before pouring, she said the Arabic blessing: In the name of God the merciful and compassionate. She tipped two small spoonfuls of sugar into each glass and stirred until the sugar dissolved, softening the tannic bite of the tea. It is the tannin in tea that brings relaxation, I've read. Drink the bitter tannin and you'll rest better. Red wine has tannin and it's that bitterness that finishes the wine. So take and drink. Enter into your rest.

Out beyond the rooftops of the neighborhood rose the mosque's golden dome and elaborate tiled minarets. The gold rotunda shone like Jerusalem's Dome of the Rock, reflecting the sun, glowing over the poor dusty surroundings. The dome burned my eyes and I couldn't look directly at it, even though, like the Ramadan moon, the mosque had no light of its own.

We sipped the tea together. Miriam told me about the hollow ache she felt when the heat of summer left the stone walls of the Old City each October, making way for chilled days, rain and sometimes snow falling directly into the courtyard. She described her longing for the days of her childhood when marriage was something that would someday enfold her and draw her into the kindness of another family. That was before she had suffered. Before she had trusted, before she had tried love and found it wanting.

She would never again allow her heart to love until she was engaged, maybe not until marriage. There was too much pain—no certainty that love would be returned. Just as she wouldn't be sure that Allah would let her into Paradise until he made his choice on the Day of Judgment, she would not be sure of a man's love until she was his bride.

Miriam knew the pain of love without promise. This was her suffering. She had been left alone. Until now, she held up a veil between her words and her heart, but our friendship had torn the partition down. Why had she chosen to reveal herself? We both knew that I, too, would betray her. In a few weeks, my study tour would be over and I would leave Damascus. I wrote nothing in my memo pad that afternoon, though she answered every question. I knew I would remember.

When I would return to Damascus those few years later, Miriam would be married to a good man, a gentle man, a poor man. She would have a son and be called Mother of Hamood. She would live in the Old City, a lane away from the family home. She would serve her husband meat once a week—lentils and tomatoes and brown beans the other days. And this man would love her. With him she would suffer in poverty, with a son and a daughter and conversation on cold nights and someone to trust until death separates. Still, she would feel the longing for something more.

EVERY YEAR THE RAMADAN MOON grows full over Damascus and then diminishes. Near the end of the month of fasting, the dim light of the aging moon holds its veil over the city. Since childhood, Miriam has gone to the roof of her Old City home on that particular night, to remember how the Koran was given, to remember that night when Allah revealed and Allah spoke. She knows that Allah does not condescend to come down, yet she aches to know and be known.

On this night, the veiled moon gives enough light for Miriam to grasp the wooden ladder, holding her Koran in her right hand, wrapped in a white cloth. Alone on the rooftop, she unwraps the Koran, kisses it, presses it to her forehead, and opens it to read.

Across the Old City rooftops, she sees the minarets rising from the big mosque that holds a shrine for John the Baptist. The southwestern spire is the Minaret of Jesus, where Damascenes say that the Prophet Jesus will first alight on the great Day of Judgment.

She wants a blessing, and she will return to the rooftop, year after year on this Night of Revelation, patient and hopeful and lonely. Miriam watches and waits for morning to split the sky from east to west. She watches for the veil to be torn, for the heavens to fall.

TRANSFORMATION CINDY BEEBE

Soldier Praying, Battle for the Rocky Crags
    —Okinawa, April 1945, photograph by W. Eugene Smith

He lies on a pallet and the pallet
on rocks and the rocks
can do nothing, it's war.
His hands touch, at the tips,
a V flipped. Or fallen,
though if you are the soldier
you can't see them,
or how the blood
splays chains of islands
over the map of your fatigues.
You see only a field of white.
Or not, perhaps your eyes

are blind behind the bandage,
so wide it's like a turban slipped
loose, slips down, soon
will overcome your mouth.
And this is how it happens.
This is how your hands,
if we tilt our heads
a little, are now a bird,
and your arms become
wings, and up, you fly up
into the heart of the lens, which
brings all things back to true.

PRELUDE NICK DUMAIS

He tastes the dry perfume of cut cedar
As sawdust spits from the fresh boards,
Split with the slow, even strokes of an arm
Knotted and perspiring, speckled with sand.

Children chatter and peek over the well
At the dusty robes and cracked toes
Of a traveling man—he smiles brightly
And lifts the hanging ladle, and drinks deep.

In the morning he will reach the sea—
He will call clearly, and they will follow.
Tonight, he rests his head on the flanks
Of a blind goat, and dreams with open eyes.

I FELL IN LOVE WITH A PREACHER'S WIFE ROSS GALE

I fell in love with a preacher's wife. The one in the novel.

She wouldn't listen to me but stays with me forever.

She sings when I sleep and I see her face in the window when the sun and rain meet for margaritas during happy hour. I smell her in the frying pan, in Chinese restaurants, in salt and sugar packets.

She would love me, I think. And I smile and then doubt. No, she would love her God and I get angry. And then me. And I smile.

She is defined by her words. They are hers and no one else's. They are mine and they are hers and they define her. They run empty hands on the small of her back, along tiny lines that dip and freckles that don't dot.

Her tears fall through me. I reach and they fall, but through mass and material into the deep wilderness of unknown breaking. Where words go to die. Where words go to die, and think, and I think something else.

Words. They die along empty roads, in garbled tones, roughed with dirt and dust and creaking rocking chairs, and gas guzzlers that don't spit, but cry oily, linear streams of children it serves and sacrifices. Handing out toys and stealing them when they're old and stressed and angry at the president.

She loves me but she's angry. And I can't save her. She lives with me forever.

My faith cries too. Their faith wipes and scoffs and mine cries. It cries for things I don't want it to cry for. Please save her.

Words die. Words die in linear streams.
What do I have left?

I have emotions and sounds. I have my native tongue and they cut it out in hatred from your father's passed down on silver pocket watches and oversized hardbacks.

What do I have?

I buy diamonds in clear windows from smiling men in suits who watch every dust bunny hop by and anticipate a slight twitch and his hand is on the button. And his brother is a scientist at your university where they made synthetic diamonds that are the real thing, where his breath bleeds fog onto its reflection of perfection.

What do I have when they copy the real thing and it's the real thing? Copy my words. Copy my words. And I'll plagiarize yours and what do we have? Words that fall in linear streams and then lie flat in dusty shelves and someone says the same thing anyways, or so similar they took it for the real thing, maybe its synthetic, but that's the real thing too.

Tears fall linear, never sideways, unless your face is in the blankets, but it's still going down. It's not like spitting out the window, where the wind carries it or jerks it back into your shoulder. And our words fall flat with cold porridge, with nervous glances, and falling eyelashes.

Words go to die in me and you and mouths wide open and hearts stabbed in gunfire and the open bar. Rum and Coke with ice and words that die holding empty wedding fingers.

What do I have?

I fell in love with a preacher's wife. The one in the novel. But I forgot to look up.

A WIFE OF NOBLE CHARACTER LINDSAY CRANDALL

Who can find a virtuous woman?
    for her price is far above rubies:

The hours swinging over
my chest, undulating,
umbrellas of bodies,
hallowed shells,
grapes without their skins.

How awkward the white—
our eyes, oyster shells—
poised, the eyes of God
eyeing us, how awkward

these reds—the stain
in the bed and roses
turn into rubies, vitreous,
luminescent stems:
a wife is made not born.

And they gather her
in her white, she blooms red,
her chromatic scales etched
into a notebook that
reads like an apothegm,
a daffodil, apologies & instructions,
a proverb, a promise,
platinum, sapphire, rust.

She sets about her work vigorously;
    her arms are strong for her tasks:

"This is a labor of love," she says,
rolling and unrolling the mud,
    years spread out and folded
like one hundred love sonnets,
some read, some unread:

Así establecidas mis razones
    de amor te entrego esta
        centuria:

Matilde, you triumphant minx,
one hundred years to give
one husband, one love,
leaning across the table
to kiss you.

She sees that her trading is profitable,
    and her lamp does not go out at night.

One way to pass the time:
wake for work each day,
each another glance
at the mirror, another shock
of her face in mine.
I hurry away
and this approximate mien
stiffens within moments.
After watering the daffodils, I
come in to put on shoes.

The work goes on:
writing more poems,
whispering more prayers,
lengthening the lines until
my breath is like a slow wind
lifting the curtain and
lowering it.

A WIFE OF NOBLE CHARACTER

She is clothed with strength and dignity;
she can laugh at the days to come.

Open the window,
she has more to say:

a penny for your company,
a thought for your shoes:

these shored-up tulips
embrace each other:

and she is clothed with strength
and dignity and

she digs into the dirt
to find a brown box:
wool, flax, vineyards,
arms, gates, bread:

her shadow extends
across the lawn:

return me here when I'm done.

Many women do noble things
  but you surpass them all:

  And I find myself
with no score to keep and
a mouthful of wifely verbs:

  And all the wives, all the
women rise, their sequined eyes,
their rubies, unmarked constellations,
their hands are maps,
where the water meets land
and

LINDSAY CRANDALL

I am here
in my husband's rough hands,
brick to brick,
north to south,
hand to hand.

AN ADAM OF MY OWN LINDSAY CRANDALL

After Eve's turn at the fruit, I took mine and
found an Adam of my own—

hair yet flaxen and biceps like carved stone, I
gave him a haircut and offered osculation—

geometry favored over a trillion stars, we
counted them all, connected their crowns—

Polaris, our didactic defender, its treatise
traces the gospels back our way.

BATHSHEBA AND THE KING LINDSAY CRANDALL

In the hour of bathing, Bathsheba
    undresses herself,
    pallor of flesh.

She is a long yellow stem
    still pink
between the legs, dropping
    her robe
from her shoulder,
    a little light scurries
across the courtyard,
    the birds clap above.

She listens to the world wrinkle,
    its noiseless pulse
unfolding like a single
    drop of blood in the ocean,
but she didn't see
    her own reflection when she
looked into
    the pool.

There the king stands
    atop the roof, adores
the fatness of her upper arm, marmalade
    of back
and Bathsheba wishes for
    a beer or a glass of Shiraz to slosh,
to glaze this temptation with glances,
tempting the fury of
    drunk love.

BATHSHEBA AND THE KING

No one knows really what she thinks
    of him,
crow on the roof, the wind blows,
    seeds diffuse.
It's spring somewhere
    in the eastern hemisphere,
and Bathsheba is summoned

    to his chamber.
She lies on a bed where many
    queens have lain,
her breasts unadorned, legs open,
    she clutches King David
and thinks of her husband
    at the city gate, his hands
clutching a weapon of destruction.

SUNSET YEARS SUZANNE RAE DESHCHIDN

for spencer ridley

beneath the heavy bear skins
frail david could not keep warm
so a maid was called to fire
his cooling embers. to rekindle
the flame, and give him heat.

naked, she slips between the
skins and wraps herself around
him. drawing him toward her.
his head upon her chest, her arms
running the length of his spine,
her fingers through his hair.

she plays with him and reminds him
of who he used to be, killer of ten
thousands. king of a nation. the
friend of God. she sees him still
in the prime of his youth, though
his strength fails. she invigorates

him. he yields to her touch. melts
into her embrace. she throws back
many skins as their heat intensifies.
he lingers in her arms, feeling her
rousing him, to life, to the fire
again.

TERMINAL JEFF NEWBERRY

For Jessica Emerson

Terminal the doctors say in their measured way
& scribble on thumb-thick stacks of white,

A clipped record of the woman's decline.
The daughter's eyes jump like an EKG.

Terminal: not a destination—a jumping-off,
An airport where commuters huff past, dragging

Black bags, squalling children. Voices announce
Arrivals, departures. A black & white screen

Ticks off destinations, gates, times. In the room,
Sheets tuck tight around her mother's body.

The white means *something*—the daughter
Can't place the symbol: death, old age, purity?

No metaphor will come. No image suffice.
Now, only a word remains:

Terminal. Cancers metastasize in the woman's mind
& soon, she's exited, baggage in tow, waving

As she leaves, her daughter's name echoing, fading
To memory, which will depart eventually, as well.

A BODY'S LAMENT JEFF NEWBERRY

I dream of a body like a clock,
Tight with wrought springs &
Spindled cogs, oiled gear teeth

Turning in mechanistic order.
I dream of a body snapped open
& disinfected hands replacing worn

Parts with factory-minted organs,
Steel & gray, still sealed, protected
From human breath & disease.

Every part replaced, new woven skin
Stretched over steel-crafted bones.
I dream of a programmed body:

Each jaw-twitch a logical consequence
Of algorithms, calculations & subroutines.
I will exhale a numbered matrix.

Tin man, you'll never understand
That black seepage is not oil. You
Won't recognize the oxidized blood rust.

You'll never feel the death in you
Pulsing like a small black bird.

SUNLIGHT SHATTERED JEFF NEWBERRY

I pray for an image, not a god
Carved of driftwood, hung

On twine, an *imago dei* beyond
Bone shards in a bloody bag.

I need more than a figured
Face on junk-store china,

Or a word-hewn god slathered
On wristbands & billboards.

More than the knowledge
Of more. More than the fall

Evenings, the barren trees
Like old men with bent backs,

Gray & dry, wrung with the work
That lay rotten about their feet,

Dug into the wormy earth:
A field of fallen leaves & limbs.

Above, sunlight falls in panes
That shatter with a sweep of my eyes.

THING PSALM: THE POET'S ACT OF CONTRITION NINA FORSYTHE

Praise God for things
that are themselves
and not objective correlatives:

for sheep that are sheep
and not meekness,

for ants that are not industry
and sloths that are not—well, sloth,

for the dovish dove
and the foxy fox
that are not peace or cunning,

for the stone
that lies in the dirt
and not in my heart,

for blue that is a color
of many lovely shades
and not a mood,

for red that is not rage or passion,
white that is not purity,
black that is not evil,
green that is neither growth nor envy,
but color, color, color, color.

It is time to stop trying
to domesticate things,

to cultivate and civilize them.
Let things be themselves for a while
without being a ding an sich,
wholly strange and wonderful.

THE RIDER AHEAD JOSEPH LAIZURE

When I was eleven, I lived for a month in a detention center called the Boys' Ranch. There weren't many moments that I was by myself, but when I was, I liked to handle a certain beaded cross necklace that I had brought with me. My friend Lane Diehl had given it to me for company, which was as much a reminder about how I got to the Boy's Ranch as it was a suggestion of what I could be when I got out. It was only on the day of my release, when my mom was two hours late in picking me up, that I noticed that the oils from my fingers had left the necklace dull and gritty. I cleaned it with my spit. I did not know it, but I would never be in trouble with the police again. I would live the next seven years being so frightened of becoming a drunk and going to jail that all my attention would be directed at keeping myself from that fate. I would get headaches and obliterate them with handfuls of aspirin, then develop an ulcer, and then begin to learn math in order to distract myself from the itching in my gut. I would excel in school because studying in the library meant I would not have to go home to do anything but sleep. I would only make friends with other children in the church. They would never drink; they would be good. I would indulge in butterscotch candies and deafening fear. Secretly, I would feel that I was better than all of my new friends, because I knew I was more afraid of God than they were and therefore loved Him more. I would tell people that God loved the world, leaving me free to hate it.

In truth, I never felt anything like love from God, nor from anyone but Lane. And I found the first piece of evidence that would lead me to this sad conclusion on a gray Saturday, the day that marked the beginning of Dad's third month in jail. I was avoiding my friends, passing most of the day on the swing set at the playground.

By the evening, I didn't feel like swinging alone anymore and went home, where I found Mom talking to Dad's brother Tony in the garage. He was climbing the stepladder and balancing a cardboard box on his shoulder while she watched him from the concrete step that led into the house. Her jeans were faded and clean, but his were filthy with gray dirt.

"Help him," she said.

"No," I said.

"Dustin," Uncle Tony grunted. "Help."

"What should I do?" I said. I stood beneath the ladder. The box swayed above me. Uncle Tony took another step up, and it creaked. I put my hands on the wooden legs, very lightly. The ladder wobbled and I pulled my hands back.

"What should I do?" I said, louder.

"Do we have another ladder?" Uncle Tony said.

"No," Mom said.

"I'm coming off this thing," he said. I got out of his way, and he backed down.

"I don't have all day," I said.

Mom leapt up from the step and grabbed my shoulder and gave me one hard shake.

"You hit me!" I said.

"I didn't hit you."

"She didn't hit you," said Uncle Tony. "You can't say things like that."

I bolted from the garage but slowed once I got out of their sight, and walked the half-mile to Lane Diehl's house. He was sitting on a basketball in his driveway, next to two other boys and his neighbor, Amy. The two boys were shooting paper-rock-scissors.

"Hey," Lane said to me. "You coming to church tomorrow?"

I nodded. He got up and bounced the ball to me.

"It's not even teams," I said.

"That's okay," Lane said. "I'm not that good."

It was a lie. Lane played much better than any of us. You could see by how tan he was that he spent all of his time outdoors playing sports. His muscles showed in his legs while he rebounded, took it back to the curb, passed to Amy, caught her pass, and performed a lay up. The other kids were thin and nimble, but I was a pink smudge. Lane and Amy kept it tied against the three of us. I thought I was having fun until I found myself guarding Lane. He stopped and started the way the pros did. I tried to stay on him, but I couldn't. After he made it past me he shot, missed, and caught his own rebound.

"We've got to go," interrupted one of the other boys.

"Next basket wins," said Lane.

"OK," said the boy. "But you gotta take it back."

Lane and I ran to the curb.

"Catch the fever!" Lane screamed and roared up the court. I saw where I could cut him off, and I made for my spot, but he wasn't there. I heard the ball falling through the net and turned to find him behind me, catching it as it came down.

Suddenly, I felt like I had been sleeping but now was awake. I pushed him into the brickwork of the garage, and he scraped his elbow against the side and dropped the ball, but he didn't fall.

"He could have hit his head," said Amy. I looked at the top row of bricks and its sharp corner. I had to turn away.

Lane didn't say anything. The other kids were calling me *fatso* and *idiot*. They were asking Lane if he was alright, which hurt me worse than the names. I stood in front of them making grunts. The sun was setting, and I didn't want to leave looking like the bad guy.

But then Lane said, "Go home, Dusty," and I knew that there was no way that I could keep from looking bad. If I said I was sorry, they'd know that I knew I'd done wrong.

So I just left. When I felt lonely, the block was always quiet and the wind was always cold.

It was dark by the time I made it back to the house. There was dinner for me on the table. Mom was watching TV, but she came to sit with me while I ate. She left the TV going in the background. It was like Dad was home.

The next morning she woke me and said that my friend was here to take me to church. In an unthinking, bleary muddle, I got dressed in nice clothes—my collared blue polyester shirt and a belt—and I went downstairs.

The Diehls' old Cadillac was idling in the driveway. I was not surprised, exactly, because even unreligious kids like me knew that Christian folks were supposed to forgive you when you did something to hurt them, but I had never seen it happen before. I opened the long, heavy door, and smelled the plastic jug odor of the car. Lane's father wore his hair slicked like a fifties singer, and Lane's mother kept hers in big blond whorls. Lane looked at ease in his Sunday outfit, which was a white shirt and a red tie. I gave a little hello and sat on the long seat next to Lane. He smiled at me. Neither of us said anything about the day before, and his parents didn't seem to be angry. He watched the road through the windshield while resting the tips of his fingers along the open window. I couldn't see if his elbow was still scraped up or not.

I had not been to church since I was a little kid, and the service didn't make much more sense to me at eleven than it did at four. Later, at the end of high school, I would silently debate with the pastor while listening. I would remember the crucial verses from his talks and compare multiple translations of them once I got to the library. I would be able to relax into the rhythm and the communality of the prayers, but for as smart as I turned out to be, when I was eleven years old, I was exceptionally rotten and dumb.

I was counting this as my first real time at church, and I was worried that my posture was bad and that I was breathing too loud. I wasn't interested in the talk that the pastor gave or even the songs. I resolved to do whatever Lane did and nothing more. But at the end of the service, the pastor asked for those who were new here and who had not yet entered into a personal relationship with Jesus to come to the altar and pray with him. I stood up, thinking I was supposed to, and I walked to the front, where the pastor, unsmiling, knelt to my height and touched my shoulders. He bowed my head even though I pushed back against him with my neck. He said a long prayer, a very long prayer. My feet hurt and I shuffled them, but I still remember the last part of the prayer, and that was, "To follow Him is to see His face in everyone." By the time he was finished, the sanctuary was empty save for the two of us and the Diehls.

In the parking lot, Lane took my shoulder and said very quietly, "You can't be too high on yourself if you want to be saved."

"I'm not," I said.

"You have to love Jesus so much that it's like you hate yourself," he said. "That's not a lesson you're supposed to hear right away but I think you're ready for it."

"I do hate myself."

"And you have to hate your parents."

"Well I don't."

"Not yet," he said. He got into the car and made room for me.

A few days later, Lane and I rode our bikes ten miles out of town to a nature reserve. He rode faster than I did, and I became tired trying not to fall any more behind. My muscles felt like they were balling up, as if they were going to split my legs like peapods and spill out on the highway. Lane got farther and farther ahead. Every now and then he'd look back and see how far behind I was. He would coast while I caught up. I wished he'd pedal as hard as he could. I was sure I'd go faster if I didn't have to worry about him seeing me.

We arrived hungry and ate sandwiches from sun-warmed plastic wrap while we stood over our bikes in the gravel lot. When we were finished, we crumbled the wrap into balls and I put both of them into my pocket. Then we ventured past the limestone blocks and into a grassy heaven.

The two of us ran through the prairie until our legs were crisscrossed by raised red scratches and dotted with black blood. At last, we flopped onto the shady side of a hill. Neither of us wore a watch, but Lane said it was time to go home.

"Can I see the inside of your house?" I said.

"Sure," said Lane.

My mom called this "inviting yourself over," and I knew it was wrong. One reason I did it anyway was that I knew the Diehls kept a separate fridge for pop in the basement, and I wanted to drink as much of it as I could, but there was another reason, too.

"Can I tell you why I don't want to go home?" I looked at him, and he said nothing and did not move. I turned away from him to watch the perfect blue sky while I explained.

My mom was an angry person. Not angry at me, but it scared me to see her mad all the time. My father was in jail because he was caught driving while he was drunk. Mom talked about how he was a stupid lout, but more than that she talked about how my Uncle Tony didn't have a life of his own and wanted to wreck ours. Tony was the one who told the police that dad drove home drunk from the Caledonia Lounge every Thursday, Friday, and Saturday night. Tony often came by with money for Mom, and when he did, she would invite him in and they would sit quietly in the kitchen and look out at the backyard garden. She told him about her tomatoes and about the rhubarb against the side of the house. Then Mom would tell him that she had to get dinner started, and he would go home.

One time he stopped by while I was home alone, and he showed me how to make brownies from a mix. We were eating them with peanut butter on top when Mom came in, and Tony didn't offer her a check that time and she told him to leave. She told me not to talk to him without her being around and then she told me that I shouldn't have made so many dirty dishes.

"And now she's going to get really mad about these scratches," I told Lane while rubbing my leg. I sat up and looked at him. His eyes were wet. He leaned towards me, and the big blue beaded cross that he wore around his neck dangled and twisted. He said, "You're welcome at my house anytime," and then he stood up.

I was in the lead as we rode home, giving hell to my creaky bicycle and trying to impress Lane, but he kept pace without even trying. The only thing worse than falling behind was getting to keep the lead out of pity.

On the way to the prairie, we had climbed a hill. Now, we were going down the same hill, and I noticed we were about to come upon a big crack on our half of the highway, a crack that spanned the shoulder where we were riding, and that looked too dangerous to try to cross with a bicycle. The only way to avoid it was to veer into the middle of the road. I looked behind me. Lane was staring into the woods, and he seemed unaware of the danger.

The right thing to do was either to slow down and wave him to a stop, or else turn toward the center of the road as early as possible so that he would follow. But I did neither of those things because I wanted him to crash. I pedaled hard, and the momentum of my pedals began to push my legs more than the other way around. Just before I would have reached the crack, I swerved around it. The glossy cornfields flashed open to both sides of me and the sky unfolded, the green and blue layers separated by dim white tassels. I breathed out, looked back. At first, I saw nothing of Lane, so I squeezed the brakes, chugged to a stop, and ditched my bike.

He was sitting part way up the hill, off the road, in the dirt. I dashed up to him and saw his bloody leg covered in bits of asphalt and gravel and sand. He was awake, looking at me, even smiling. His bike leaned against the guard rail. The chain ring was wet with his blood and the front wheel had tacoed. His hands were bloody and one of his cheeks was scraped.

"Dusty, I went right into that crack," he said joyfully.

"Your leg," I said.

"Will you just help me with my bike? I'll wash the sand out of the cuts when we get home."

I wrested the frame up, but it wobbled on the mangled wheel. Lane walked ahead of me. I said, "Maybe I should have warned you."

"Come on, keep up," Lane said. "I'm not hurt."

He walked to my bike, lifted it upright, and started pushing while leaning over the handlebars. Lane was a hardy kid. In the three months I had known him, he had told me about the times he slipped off of his roof, fell through the ice next to a culvert, and walked three miles in a blizzard for fun. I didn't think he was hurt until he began staggering.

"I could have told you about the crack," I said. I was crying.

He didn't turn around right away. We kept walking. Then he stopped and said, "Well, why didn't you warn me? You didn't give a damn if I crashed." It was the first time he had ever sworn in front of me.

"You could have gone around it if you weren't so cocky."

"Don't use that kind of language!" he shouted. Spit flew off his lips and pricked me.

He threw down my bike, bent over, and rubbed his hand along his hurt leg, gathering the wet pebbles that had stuck to him. With a perfect wind-up, he whipped the pebbles into the corn. Then I pushed his bicycle into the ditch.

We stood, slouching at each other. Cars and semi trucks passed us and rattled the road. There were voices in the cornfields. Some people who sounded like high-schoolers were working in there, yanking on the stalks.

Lane was now kneeling on the crust of the highway. His eyes widened, soaking up the pain. I said, "My mom has bandages that she can put on your leg. If you come back to my house, she'll let you have some."

Lane's voice wavered. "I need them now. Besides, we've got them too. Besides, it hurts too much to get back." He lay down in the ditch. "Hear those guys in the cornfield? Will you ask them to help us?"

I didn't wait. I broke through the corn and found one of the older guys. I said that my friend was hurt, and he answered that he'd get a truck.

When I got back, Lane asked, "Are they harvesting the corn?"

"No, I think they're ripping off the tassels." I heard a crow. I saw something shining on the road but it disappeared. I sat next to him and put my fingers in his hair.

A red pickup emerged from a hidden gravel road and crawled toward us, tilting as it rode the shoulder and the grassy ditch. Some syrupy odor was everywhere. The sun was instantly covered by clouds, and the air felt cooler.

The looks on the faces of the high-schoolers scared me as they hurried toward Lane, swearing. Just before they came upon us, I looked Lane in the eyes and said, "We could work in the corn together when we get to high school."

"Go to hell," Lane said.

After he was dropped off at the emergency room, I was taken home in the truck. Lane was all I thought about that awful evening. He was good in every way. He gave away the treats that his mother packed in his lunch. He didn't allow anyone around him to say bad words, or even things like *cocky*, *gosh*, or *screwed up*. Earlier in the summer he had made the game of marbles popular again, but he never played for keeps because it was unchristian. When once we sat on his parents' porch and drew pictures with crayons, I made a naked woman and he tore up my drawing.

Now I had hurt that good boy. I wanted to visit him in the hospital, and I waited alone in our garage, chalking a huge spiral on the concrete floor while my mom asked permission from Lane's parents. Mom came out and sat on the step, showing no sign of being angry. Instead, she looked bored with me.

"Mrs. Diehl says you are not allowed."

"Am I in trouble?" I asked.

"What do you think?"

"I think I am."

"You think you are," she said. I felt that it was wrong for me to be holding such a childish thing as a piece of blue chalk.

The next day the hospital released Lane. Even before he had eaten lunch at his own house, he came to my door and stood before me, displaying his dark, jeweled scabs, and he said, "I found out there's free butterscotch hard candy at the emergency room. Want to go get some?" I didn't say anything. We just headed out on foot, Lane striding as though he had never been hurt at all.

That afternoon, over the bowl of butterscotches in the emergency room lobby, I asked Lane if he wanted to see the place where my Uncle Tony worked, which was also where my Dad used to work.

We met in a ditch at the city limits at dark. I led him to the construction site, which was just outside town where there weren't many streetlights, only the four of them that lit the silent highway. The sound of a truck backing into a loading dock rumbled at us from a mile away. There were farmhouses silhouetted in the glow of distant towns. Lane and I climbed onto the backhoe. He crouched on one of the hubs, and I was in the cab. I was trying to pull a wire out of its guide. Lane was watching without speaking. I got it free and took my wire cutter from my jeans.

"Dusty," Lane said.

I snipped the wire, stripped off some insulation, and touched the bare end of it to the metal edge of the cab. I smiled at the resulting blue sparks.

"Dusty," he said, "don't do that any more."

"It's fun," I said, and ran the sparking wire around the cab. Its buzz pleased me.

"This isn't fun," he said.

"You can go if you want."

He grabbed my wrist. The way he did it took all the strength out of me and I dropped the wire to the rubber floor. I thought he was going to tell me to quit it, but he didn't start with that, not exactly. He said, "Your dad never got saved. That's why he was sent up. He drinks and drives only because he wasn't saved by Christ Jesus. Do you understand that?"

"Yes," I said. I just wanted to say whatever would make him want to let me go.

He put his hands on my shoulders. "Do you want to be saved?"

"Yes."

He bowed his head and I watched him. He started to pray for me, then looked up. "Bow your head, Dusty," he said. He began again. He told God that I knew Jesus was my savior. We both said *amen*.

We looked at each other, and he let go of me. His friendly face was all sweaty.

"You're so gullible," I said.

Lane's eyes became dull. His feelings seemed to be shutting down one by one. I wanted him to hit me so we'd be even. I thought he would spring at me and I waited for him to do it, but he stayed perched on the hub. I started to hear his breathing. Lane smelled of Tater Tot hotdish.

Slowly, I brought the wire up from the floor and let its frayed metal tip dangle in the air between us. A jerk of my wrist, and the tip swung toward his face. He didn't move. I thought about whipping him with the tip. But as long as I thought about it I wouldn't do it. It was only when I stopped thinking that Lane would be in real danger. My feet were sweating, and I adjusted my balance.

And then Lane was holding the wire. He had taken it so delicately that I didn't even know if he had lifted it from my fingers before I shuffled my feet or after. I backed away from him, moving further into the cab.

He held the tip close to his open palm. "You want to see me get shocked?"

"Do it," I said.

He waited. In my imagination I saw smoke coming off of him.

"Don't," I said.

"Too late," he said. But he didn't move. Then: "You know I can't be hurt." I shifted until I was in the middle of the vinyl seat. I didn't let any part of me touch anything that was metal. He said, "Where are your hands, Dusty?" I held them up.

He brought the tip of the wire to the frame of the cab. It snapped and buzzed, and in the blue light I saw his suddenly eager face and it scared me more than I've ever been scared.

"Still works," he said. He held the tip to his neck.

"You'll get hurt."

"If I get hurt, tell my parents it wasn't your fault."

"They won't believe me."

"You don't think so?"

"No. Quit it."

"I guess you've hurt me before." He made the wire dance near his neck and his face.

"Quit it!" I pounded the seat.

"Pray to Jesus that I stop."

"No."

He brought the wire next to his wrist again. "That's the only way I'm gonna stop."

"Please don't."

Then he touched the wire to his wrist. When he got shocked, there was a bang from somewhere off to the side. Lane bounded backward off from the hub and landed in the dirt first on his feet and then on his butt.

"Hooo," he said. The wire lay next to him.

From the underside of the backhoe, where the bang had come from, I now heard a sound like the scrabbling of insects.

"Lane, get up!" I screamed.

"I'm gonna," he said. "Just wow." He sat up. "What's that sound?"

Then I figured it out. "You blew up the battery," I said. A light came on outside a farmhouse. "This is my Uncle Tony's," I said. "It's not his but he uses it. We can't wreck it. I'm dead."

Lane picked up a fallen branch, and threw it into the trees. He laughed. He hopped into a patch of moist dirt and splattered his own legs with it. He began walking away toward the gravel road

"Hey!" I said. "Are you going to tell your parents what we did?"

"I have to. If I didn't, I'd be lying."

His shoes crunched gravel until he got to the street, and then I heard the lone tap of a stray pebble. After that, I didn't hear him at all. I sat in the cab for as long as I could stand it. I believed I was going to go to jail. I didn't want to go to jail, so I prayed. My prayer was a long, mumbling list. I asked for Dad to come home and be immune from getting drunk, for Uncle Tony to go the hell away, and for Mom to be nice. I asked to be smart. I asked to be strong like Lane. I wanted Jesus to make me nice, too. But most of all I didn't want to get in trouble for wrecking the backhoe.

My jaw hurt. I stopped praying and crying. I was relieved, but after I slipped my wire-cutter in my pocket and hopped down, I felt embarrassed. I didn't want to be the kind of kid who prayed all the time and who was weak, too. It had to be one or the other. I was going to walk home.

I started crying again and felt that Jesus was walking next to me with an arm around my shoulders, and that God was on the other side with his arm around me, too. I held up both my arms on their invisible shoulders and I cried and walked. I was walking toward the highway when the cruiser pulled off the road and stopped before me, his high beams making me turn away, warming me up.

Both Lane and the cop got out of the cruiser. They walked past me. The headlights lit up the battery compartment, which had gone green, white, and lumpy.

"You boys did this?" he said.

"Well, he did," said Lane. He was looking away, off into the dark of the field and the white light outside the farmhouse.

I have never been able to discern whether or not God loved me, but I knew that Lane did, and this, his toughness, his will to mar his own soul with a lie, this was love.

WHAT WOULD JESUS WEAR JENNA RISANO

saturday morning. somewhere there was a cartoon on
    i missed it.

Sister spoke in short sentences that began with full names
    —say it.

squeezing faith from burgundy beads i called Mary
    for the first time.

"fruit of thy *loom*, Jesus" and i hit the floor
    face beading, tears ringing, the lesson blurred before me:

know your latin, know your place, and never ask—

    what's underneath?

STONING, SOUTHERN BAPTIST STYLE ELLEN HERBERT

ONE JULY SUNDAY IN 1963 I was sitting in our church sanctuary a few minutes before the service when I sensed a strange energy in the air. Little did I know that what I was about to witness would remain with me the rest of my life. I was a young teen then, and this was the second summer I had been babysitting. Two months earlier our church had gotten a new minister, Reverend Tuck. You may wonder what my babysitting had to do with the new minister's arrival, yet these two seemingly dissimilar facts are entwined in my memory for good reason.

When I began to babysit, I began to snoop through the houses of people who hired me to care for their children. Most of my customers were from our church. As with most sin, I slipped into snooping gradually, starting with a lady's old high school yearbook I found one night when I was bored. I read stuff her classmates had written. *Oh Gloria you're such a doll. Never change a thing about yourself. Roses are red, violets . . .* Yearbook messages have never been interesting, yet reading these banalities was a short leap to reading people's mail.

What drove me to comb these houses once I got the kids down for the night? Maybe I sought knowledge I could not find in my World Book Encyclopedias. Or maybe I was trying to prove my pet theory that people were not who they presented themselves to be. Although I felt guilty about snooping and promised myself I would stop, it became an addiction. Years later I would discover that my sister Laura, also a babysitter, snooped too, so maybe it's an inherited trait.

For most of the previous summer, I had not found anything amiss about the Honeycutts. They appeared to be perfect Baptists, since Mr. H. was a deacon and his wife Caroline a stay-at-home mom, the opposite of my own family of imperfect Baptists. My dad only attended church when he'd gotten in some scrape and was trying to atone to Mother, a high school English teacher.

"Their house is so cold I need a sweater," I told my best friend Vonda over the phone the night I discovered the Honeycutts' secret.

The Honeycutts lived at the country club in an all-electric house with central air conditioning, a big deal in the 1960s. Their house was also sealed off from the outside world, so that sounds were muffled, something that would be important later.

"Quit bragging," Vonda said, "and get to work." She was my partner in snooping. I promised to call her back if I found anything juicy.

I went down the hall, passing little Samantha's room. She was two years old and always asleep when I babysat. The perfect baby to go with the perfect family.

The door to their bedroom was ajar. I had decided not to bother looking in there, since I had combed their room on other occasions. Yet I noticed something under their bed. Between the dust ruffle and the floor was a package.

I knelt and retrieved it. The package was wrapped in brown paper and its typed label addressed to Mr. Honeycutt, its return address a post office box in New York City. By feeling it, I knew the package was a paperback, which surprised me. Except for Bibles and Sunday school publications, the Honeycutts had few books. I had assumed they weren't readers, but I must have been wrong.

Since obviously I couldn't open the package, I lifted the dust ruffle and put it back where I'd found it. As I did so, I noticed something odd: a low squat bookshelf under their bed filled with paperback books.

I have thought back on this many times and wished I hadn't seen the bookshelf because once I did there was no stopping me.

I flattened against the floor so I didn't bump my head on the bed frame and reached under. I took hold of a book.

"Feels wonderful in here," I told Mrs. Honeycutt one Saturday night the next summer when I had come to babysit. Outside the temperature hovered around one hundred degrees, the air soupy with humidity.

Caroline Honeycutt smiled and fingered her strand of pearls. She was a thin woman with lacquered hair that was never out of place. "There are Pepsis in the fridge and all the makings for ham sandwiches. Help yourself, dear."

I had begun imagining her as a character in one of the books under the bed, wearing only her pearls, and instantly I felt ashamed of myself. She was always nice to me.

"We're going to the Moore's for dinner," she said and waved a piece of paper. "Here's their number."

The Moores, another well-off family from Tar River Baptist, also lived at the country club.

Mr. H. was outside in their Cadillac, waiting for Caroline, who strode to the door, then turned. "In case I forget later, could you ask your mother to give me a call? Tell her it's church business."

"Sure." I knew what *church business* she meant.

Some of the deacons along with other members were upset that our new preacher's wife had been married before.

"Don't they have anything better to do?" Mother had asked when she got an invitation in the mail to attend their secret meeting. She threw it in the trash, where I retrieved it when she wasn't looking.

The invitation said that certain Tar River Baptist members felt concerned about the new direction the church was taking, so they had called this secret meeting to explore other possibilities. Below Yours in Christ were the signatures of our more prosperous members, including the Moores and Honeycutts.

An image of Reverend Tuck's wife, Mary, dark-haired and curvaceous with a peaches and cream complexion, came to me. So what if she had been married and divorced before she met and married the Reverend? How could her past life possibly affect these church members? They must be jealous of Mrs. Tuck's beauty or possibly her lovely singing voice. The choir director, admiring her full, rich soprano, had invited her into the choir, where she had already sung several solos.

After Mrs. Honeycutt left, I checked on Samantha, who was asleep as usual. After I ate a sandwich, I wandered down the hall to their bedroom and discovered the latest addition to their library, *Women Behind Bars*. I took the book to the hallway to read.

I use the word read loosely. None of their books had much story. Yet because the eyes of the people in them had been darkened so the reader could not identify them, the characters resembled raccoons. Since all the people in all the books had these same blacked-out eyes, I came to think of the books as a series, the adventures of the naked raccoon people.

This latest book made me laugh. A woman with immense breasts pressed them against prison bars. Her dark nipples looked like eyes peering out from her chest. A prison guard, shorter and smaller than she, held a whip high over his head and wore a silly smile that was supposed to look sinister.

I had to tell Vonda about this one. I took the book to the kitchen and dialed from their wall phone.

As the phone was ringing, I heard Mrs. Honeycutt on the porch. They were about to open the front door!

I froze.

"Hello," Vonda said, awakening me to the fact that I had to get rid of that book, that I did not have time to go to their bedroom, and replace it in the bookshelf.

I put down the phone and darted into the hall as they pushed open the front door.

Vonda and I would go over the next moments often. Every time we did, she wondered why I didn't stick the book in my shoulder bag, which was large enough to conceal it.

"That would have been stealing," I told her.

Instead I entered the first door I came to, baby Samantha's room. As I closed the door behind me, I heard them in the living room.

I had to do something fast.

Beside Samantha's crib was a wicker basket filled with Golden Books. I picked up *Three Billy Goats Gruff*, threw in *Women Behind Bars*, and put the Golden Book back on top.

"Ellen?" Mrs. Honeycutt called softly.

I opened the door and stepped into the hall.

Both Honeycutts stood there looking at me. My heart became so loud I was afraid they could hear it pounding.

"I thought Samantha was crying," I said, "so I went in to check on her."

Mr. H. nodded, but Caroline looked suspicious. She strode past me into Samantha's room.

At that moment what I had done hit me. I had put that filthy book beside their sleeping child. I was disgusted with myself and afraid. They were sure to find it.

Caroline Honeycutt might be discovering *Women Behind Bars* at this moment. She might run out of the room with it and confront me. But she didn't.

She walked out, smiling. Samantha was fine. That was all she was thinking about.

Mr. Honeycutt drove me home and tipped me as usual.

I could not sleep that night, thinking about the moment when they found the book. Samantha was walking now, but they would not believe that she had toddled into their bedroom, picked up the newest addition to their porn collection, and brought it back to her room to peruse.

I dreaded going to church, where I would have to see them. I tried to get out of going, but Mother made me go.

"Did they say anything to you?" Vonda asked Sunday afternoon.

"No, which means they haven't found the book yet. But once they do—who knows? Could they have me arrested?"

Vonda laughed. "I think pornography is against the law in North Carolina. So they would get themselves arrested if they reported you."

With our bikinis on under our clothes, we were walking down Preston Road to the

Holiday Inn, our home away from home. The desk clerks knew we weren't guests, but they didn't mind our presence around the pool.

Yet not even an afternoon of swimming and diving quelled my nervous stomach or my fear that was building. The worst part was not knowing what the Honeycutts would do to me.

I discovered the answer on Tuesday when Mrs. Moore called.

I listened to Mother's side of the conversation. "Sorry, Louise," Mother said. "Laura's at the beach, so she can't babysit for you, but Ellen's standing right here. Would you like to speak to her?"

I held my breath as my mother's expression changed to one of curiosity. "Okay. Sure. Bye now." She hung up.

"That's funny," Mother said to me. "When I told her that you could babysit for them, she said no thanks."

Fortunately Mother's curiosity was bound by time constraints. She wanted to finish reading *The Daily News* before she had to get dinner on. So she let the matter drop.

I went to my room and sprawled across my bed as what had happened sunk in. I hated the anti-climax of it, the lack of resolution. I realized the Honeycutts would never openly confront me.

"They've blackballed me," I told Vonda. "My babysitting career is over."

I imagined the Honeycutts having another secret meeting to alert church members to the fact that I was a snooping babysitter. I figured I would never get another good babysitting job in town again, but I was wrong. Like my darling dad, my luck is boundless.

BACK TO THAT SULTRY SUNDAY MORNING when the church sanctuary buzzed with an evil energy. Every pew was packed with people, unusual for mid summer. Laura, Mother, and I sat with the Barnes's family toward the back of the church.

Reverend Tuck came to the podium, opened his Bible, and marked a passage he would read later.

After a hush fell over the congregation, a tense silence followed. I noticed the Honeycutts sitting on the front row. At the sight of them, my stomach went into a free fall. Beside them were their pals, the Moores, an overfed bunch who took up the rest of the pew.

The members of the secret committee filled all the front pews. They were dressed up, the women in linen dresses and hats, the men in suits and ties. And in this church with no air conditioning and only a few giant fans strategically placed.

As the choir in black robes entered the choir box behind the altar, the front pews began to stir. Once Mrs. Tuck entered in the middle of the choir, the secret committee members stood, the women with purses dangling from their wrists, the men with a child in arms or one by the hand.

Without saying a word, they filed out of their pews and lined up in the aisle to leave. They were shunning her! I saw in their faces that if we had lived in the time of stoning, they would have gathered rocks for this occasion.

Leading their procession after the Moores was Mr. Honeycutt, Samantha in his arms. As he walked down the aisle, his eyes met mine. He sent me a stinging look. To spite him, I held his gaze and would not allow myself to look away. How righteous he appeared, hugging his daughter.

Caroline came behind him, her head down as if she was ashamed. Maybe she was ashamed of what she was doing today. Or maybe she was ashamed of what I knew about them.

Whatever the case, I was glad she did not look at me. I am sorry for hurting her. I always believed that she was basically a decent person married to a bastard.

Not that he was a bastard because he read porn. I've got nothing against it. As a writer, I believe censorship of any kind is unacceptable in a democracy. His hypocrisy made him a bastard. Whatever he told the Moores and others about me, he had not told them the truth: that I had gotten into his pornography collection. This made me wonder what he had told them, perhaps that I had stolen something from them. In a way that was true. I had stolen their secret.

The foyer of the church was not carpeted, so their footsteps against the hardwood floor echoed inside the sanctuary. After the church doors slammed behind them, we sat in silence, not quite believing what had happened.

THIS INCIDENT MADE SUCH AN IMPRESSION on me that I have written it in fiction as well. I tell my writing students that there are stories we need to tell, and this is one of mine. At the time this occurred I had seen my dad's drunken friends do stupid crazy things, dance inappropriately, walk into a closed door, clean fish and put a knife through an unsteady hand. But this was Sunday morning, and these were sober church people, God's people. I had believed they were safe.

I'm not sure what lesson I took from the secret committee. I could say: beware of the self-righteous, of organized religion, and mobs, since people in herds do outrageously cruel things they would not do individually. But I'm still not sure that's it. The wonderful thing about creative writing is that the writer does not have to fully understand in order to write about an incident. In fact I believe our best material comes from things not understood. That way writing is a process of discovery for writer as well as reader.

* * *

Our congregation sat listening to their cars turn one-by-one onto Preston Drive and their engines fade away. Later we would learn that the entire secret committee moved their membership to First Baptist.

Someone, maybe it was Mr. Barnes or maybe it was Mother, got up and moved to that first empty pew. The rest of the church followed until the front of the church was filled in front.

Essentially that's what happened in the months and years ahead. The people left behind assumed leadership roles the secret committee members had held. The Honeycutts and the Moores had been big fish in our little pond. At First Baptist, they were still big fish, just not as big as they had been to us.

During this process of them departing and us migrating to the front, Reverend Tuck stood as if paralyzed, his face having assumed a stricken look.

He was a bright man and ambitious. In the years ahead he would double our church membership and improve our finances to the point that a huge new sanctuary with central air conditioning would be built, a structure rivaling First Baptist's. We would get our own baptismal well and not have to use theirs any more. He was even elected to the City Council. No telling what heights he might have reached if he hadn't died young of a heart attack while helping plant azaleas on the church lawn.

Although he knew his scripture and could deliver a powerful sermon, he was a cold man. He did not visit the sick easily nor could he loosen his tie and become jovial at church suppers. He wasn't really the kind shepherd Tar River Baptist needed. The best thing the Reverend ever did was to love his wife Mary. And that hour she was publicly rebuked was his finest.

Once he came to his senses, he turned from us and extended his hand to her. "Mary," he called her in a whisper we all heard.

He got her to come down from the choir box and stand beside him. Tears shone in her eyes, but she held herself erect. He delivered his short sermon with his arm around her waist, perhaps realizing for the first time the trouble he had brought her when he had asked her to marry him, a Baptist minister. He had put her at the mercy of the Moores, the Honeycutts, and others of their ilk, moneyed, self-righteous people, whose own lives could not stand up under the scrutiny they gave others.

During his sermon, I thought about the Honeycutts and how their departure affected me. Me, me, me. I was a teenager, self-absorbed in the extreme. I realized that whatever the Honeycutts had told their friends about me, it was going with them.

Not that I was off the hook entirely. This was Jacksonville, North Carolina, so I was bound to run into them or hear about them from others, and every time I did, a wave of shame would wash over me. What I had done would be with me for the rest of my life.

Yet sitting in church that morning I was not sorry I had snooped, only that they had caught me. In my process of discovering their secret, they had discovered mine. Instead of never snooping again, I resolved to be more careful. But a year or so later, I did stop. I wasn't interested any more. Snooping was a sin I outgrew.

LITTLE GIRLS J. MARCUS WEEKLEY

a response to Fairchild

Their light bodies lift the sewn speech
of breathe and push and glorious newborns
imagined, waiting for flesh. Their blushes, despite
formulas of unknown chemistry,

blood clouds their smooth faces.
On the swings their mouths and eyes
giggle as they swear against
sterility. Then, the click of tooth

against tooth, lips lacquered but
unprepared to speak, to breathe,
into another. In their wondering
and quick steps, do they hear

Mom, Dad argue over meatloaf,
notice his arm around her during church,
imagine them at night? And after Science,
after Math, they speak together

about tiny hands, milk bottles,
breasts as big as softballs. One
in a pink princess shirt says to her unreal prince,
Marry me. I want three babies.

And her near-forgotten book shows a hero,
clad in shiny silver, carrying a sword
too heavy for a real man. But
she pictures their first son, the second,

a girl with blond pigtails. Mom
says it's time for bed, and the princess
prays for smooth skin, kids as sweet
and kind as she is.

PRODIGAL LYNN DOMINA

Years afterward, he glanced at a crudely
formed bowl, noticed the knot of cucumber peels
floating in brine, brown and white eggshells
heaped together, waste
ready for pigs though his family
kept no pigs. Nearly sinking
to the ground, he remembered his sin
against God and the father who forgave
too prodigally. He feared his father's assurance—
that such months scavenging for scraps,
his skin thick with sweat and shame,
sufficed as penance. He longed
for anger, a voice
raised in accusation. Some afternoons,
passing sheep at their leisurely grazing,
he yearned yet to be off, to seduce, be seduced,
feel his belly full of wine.
What of it? He would never
work off the debt of his first betrayal
or forget scrambling after husks, wilted pods,
moldy crusts. Once a chunk of pomegranate
had clung to its rind, nearly spoiled,
so unbearably sweet the flavor
consumed his awareness of himself
kneeling with pigs.

PREGNANT AND UNWED ON A SMALL CHRISTIAN CAMPUS IN KIRKLAND, WASHINGTON HOLLY CARTER

I'm no longer that person
you used to look up to.
I'm no longer that girl
you admire.
Now I'm just "that girl."

HUNDRED DOLLAR BILLS LINDA MCCULLOUGH MOORE

So I guess I'm not what you'd call a charity junkie. I come by my condition honestly, my mother was the *Yes* queen. I mean, I'd come home from school to find she'd given away my new winter coat to some freezing kid and she would put me in the car and take me down to Goodwill to get a replacement only she'd feel guilty taking some coat some other poor kid could use and so we'd end up at Steigers where she'd end up paying twice what the first one cost plus we see these Looney Tunes underpants, six bucks apiece and she'd buy me three of these for being such a sport. On the way home we'd stop off at the A&P and spend fifteen minutes looking for these coated pecans that's she's crazy for, and then she'd drop them in a survival center food bin on the way to the car. *I will not give to the Lord that which costs me nothing*, she'd say. She'd sneak up to the ladies who cleaned the toilets in the bathrooms in some public building—she wouldn't let me go alone to the men's room till I was twelve—and she'd slip the lady a twenty folded up real small and tell her that her work was important to a lot of people. And my dad would sneak back into a hotel room to pocket three quarters of the money that she left the maid.

I'm not a bit like her, but at least I'm not like him. She said a person couldn't outgive God, but from where I was sitting she sure gave it her best shot.

So I have a congenital giving aversion, although I'm honest to a fault. That's why it shocks me how I react when I first find the money. I'm in this antique store with Martha, this woman I met at the vet's about a month ago. She's got one of the nastiest dogs I've ever seen, a dog she's nuts about. I've got probably the sweetest tempered beagle on the planet, and I've had about a hundred separate fantasies of his demise. I don't want him to be dead, it's just I don't want him to be mine, or not forever. I'm not a dog person, if such a thing is possible for someone who has never been without a dog for one day in his life. I guess maybe I just want to know what it feels like to wake up in the morning and not have a dog. To go out for a walk, all by myself. My sister Jenny says it just means I'm afraid of losing, afraid of death, so I pretend I want it, but she doesn't get it. I don't want Henry, that's the beagle, dead, I just want him gone away. Henry was the last dog my mother had. I can't get rid of him. It would be like getting rid of her.

Martha goes up front to ask the owner what he wants for this antique handmade statue of ebony. That's when I open up this huge wooden box and beneath some crumpled newspaper I see the money. A tight roll wrapped in a hundred dollar bill. I turn my back to the front of the stall ands loosen the wrapped bills, all hundreds. The thing's the size of a Coke can. I can't believe the owner didn't see it. I can't believe I did. I notice approximately nothing.

"He wants $45," Martha says, "And the pinky's broken off at the knuckle."

Somehow without any help from me the roll of bills has found its way into my jacket pocket.

"Would you like it?" I say. "Do you mind the finger's missing?"

"I don't mind, but that's way too much."

And I imagine peeling off a hundred dollar bill and tossing it toward the owner, pointing to the maimed hand, telling him to keep the change, telling Martha it was nothing. Taking her to some swanky nightclub, in the middle of the afternoon, and creasing bills the long way to hand to maitre d's and waiters and cigarette girls, if they still have them. I don't think I'd actually buy much. You don't with cash. You don't buy things. You flash the bills around and give twelve silver dollars to some kid.

The owner scowls at us and starts back the crowded aisle towards us. "Forty," he says. "I could do forty, it's what I paid for it."

Martha smiles. Her dog may be hell on wheels but she sure has a nice smile. "Oh that's all right, I think I've changed my mind. Thanks all the same."

My mother would have bought it, would have paid full price, would have taken it home and given it pride of place on the mantle and then passed it off to the first person who admired it.

You never knew from day to day around the house whether a thing was just misplaced or had been given to the Amway representative.

I clench my fingers tighter around the roll of bills, studying the tall man's face for signs of canny cunning, some hint that he has planted the bills for a trap. Or did God do that?

Or the devil?

"We should go," Martha says. "I have to work at six."

"Yes, we'll be leaving now," I say and stop just short of winking at the man.

He doesn't know about the roll of bills. There's not a subtle bone in this guy's body.

"I'd say you've got some real money in this place," I say and look him straight in the eye.

"People don't get it," he says. "You gotta tie up cash in inventory, real cash."

"I know," I say. "I know."

Martha makes her way down the long aisle, stopping once to pick up an ashtray that looks like one made by some kid at camp. "I always wanted to have a little boy," she says and it occurs to me I may have cash enough to buy her one on the black market. If they still have that. In sixty years a person can get so out of touch if you don't pay close attention, keep up with the changes.

I grasp the bills and give a squeeze; there's not much give. I turn my collar up, and we go outside. There is no squad car waiting at the curb, no siren sound, no alarm, no one waving a gun and running after us.

I spot a homeless guy down by the corner.

I think I'll make him guess which hand.

IS ANYONE ALL RIGHT? LINDA MCCULLOUGH MOORE

I would kill for a cup of coffee. I'm sitting in a movie theater beside a stranger—well a stranger to me—a man I met online, the single stupidest place to meet a person in the history of the world.

It gets worse.

The couple sitting in the row behind us met the same way, I'm almost certain. There are conversations people have when they first meet in person after days or weeks of email-fabricated flippancy and wild invention that resemble real life conversation in no way.

"Do you have any hobbies?" my seatmate whispers, louder than is strictly speaking necessary.

"I have my own chain saw." These words spoken, as if in reply, in a husky woman's voice originating from directly behind me. I should have thought to move my lips, let her ventriloquize.

"I cut fifty cords of wood last year," her mate replies. A match made in heaven. They're both drunk, as far as I can tell—shared interests figure largely in online dating— and when the lights go down and I can turn around, I expect to see that they both resemble no one so much as one another.

"Do you have any hobbies?" my date asks in the same voice he used the first time.

"I don't think so," I say. It comes out sounding rude. Truth does that. A lot. But I'm not positive I do or don't. The only thing that comes to mind is stamp collecting which I don't, in any intentional way, and I'm afraid if I said yes, he'd ask me what my hobby was. I already have him pegged as someone who follows facts back home to their burrows, and stands there, patient all night long if need be, till the truth comes up for air.

I'm pretty sure we two aren't soul mates. In fact, I'm not convinced we're slated to make it through the movie. I keep trying to figure how impolite it would be to leave him for a cup of coffee in the café across the street.

"I don't have any hobbies either." He sounds bereft. My first thought is to fix him up with the couple behind us. If he can't chop wood, surely he could learn to drink. I did once. Now that's a hobby. I unlearned it though. Now I just think of drinking, and I mainline caffeine and walk wired through life.

"Would you like to do something after the movie?" he says.

"Well, let's just see how late it goes," I say. I know full well it ends at 9:05. I always know beforehand when a thing will end.

The lights go down, the sound goes up, I feel a bass beat in my inner ear. The floor thumps.

"Stop that!" the chainsaw lady giggles and spills what smells like popcorn on my shoulders. "Oops, sorry about that, lady."

"No problem." I turn fully in my seat and face a child. She can't be more than twenty. I'm sixty-two. I could make three of her and change. Her match mate looks too old to remember much of forty.

My first impulse is to take her by the hand and lead her down the orange-light-bulb-lighted stairs, out of the dark, out into the summer evening.

"Fuck," she says. More giggles. "Oops, I didn't mean you." She buries her face in the man's jacket and the laughing sounds like she is struggling to breathe.

"Would you like popcorn?" Bob—my seatmate, give him a name—asks me.

"I'm pretty sure I don't," I say, too equivocal, once more.

"No thank you," I wax definitive, move from mean to stiff.

The screen is full of penguins which I'm pretty sure I'm phobic of. I close my eyes and hope I've come to see some other movie. I thought it was about a plane crash and football, but I only skimmed the listing. I could have overlooked the penguin part. Once you're afraid, really afraid, of anything, it's everywhere you go.

A chirping comes from somewhere underneath my seat and I lift both feet off the floor, eyes still closed, heart pumping. If there is one thing I fear more than penguins, it is things that chirp under people's seats in darkened theaters you thought were inhabited by nothing more harmful than lonely, online daters looking for love in all the wrong places.

The chirp again. I open my eyes and Bob appears to be frisking himself, then he extracts what can only be a cell phone from a jacket pocket and starts jabbing at it, making sounds I take for disgruntlement, but which may well be asthma.

The screen goes black and for a minute I think the movie's over, then as quickly remember that it hasn't started yet. Bob stuffs his cell phone somewhere, breathing heavier than I find entirely appealing, and the drunk lumberjacks behind me between them manage to produce a sloshing sound like water in a large tank. It doesn't bear thinking.

Now we're on a football field, or the actors on the screen are. Bob and I and the match-made-in-heaven breathing down our necks are much as we have ever been and I think will ever be, playing on a field not half so level, or well-marked, protected by neither helmets nor shoulder pads, clearly members of no team.

We already know that every player on the field will, before the popcorn's done, board an airplane, cheer in unison, drink cokes, eat peanuts, and then die. And we know that after that will come the triumph of the human spirit. I hate the triumph of the human spirit. Especially because it so often follows a planeload of teenagers' dying in a fiery crash.

And still we come to the movies. And still we sit and every time expect the show to end some other way.

"Are you all right?" Bob spit-whispers in my ear.

"Sure," I say.

"I just wondered," he says and he starts his frisking thing again, though in response to no chirping sounds I hear, but then, the football game has gotten pretty rowdy, the cheerleaders, I think, overreaching. I mean, the team is Division III.

Bob fidgets with the buttons on his cell phone which emits a blue light that's as offensive as a noise. The drunk woman behind us sighs in transport. I hear a Velcro ripping sound. The opposing team on the screen—many of whom will live to ripe—overripe—old age—scores a touchdown. And one of the good guys lies on the muddy field, down for the count.

"Are you all right?" Bob asks again.

"I'm just going to go out and grab a coffee," I whisper. "I'll be right back."

"Shhhhhh," somebody whispers.

"Absolutely," I say out loud.

"Should I come with you?" Bob says.

"No," I say. "Stay here."

Somebody needs to man the phone.

I crawl over Bob, the long-life players make another touchdown, the chainsaw woman moans. I look back but it's too dark to see if she is as naked as I imagine. I wave at Bob. He's patting his coat pocket.

Once outside, the air is fine. It's a good evening for football. I should go back in and rally everybody in the place to come outside and play a pick-up game of flag—or tackle—ball. Someone surely has a football in their trunk. Or, for sure, they should.

Getting a cup of coffee takes approximately forever. There's a line and every coffee has six ingredients that have to be discussed in some detail.

I sneak my coffee back inside by pulling my arm up higher in my sleeve until neither the cup nor my hand is visible. The hot liquid sloshes, dousing half my sleeve, and for the rest of what will be this querulous evening, every time I raise my arm I'll catch a whiff of stale caffeine.

"Are you all right?" Bob says as I slide past him.

"Hummm," I hum.

"I thought you got arrested."

I try to conjure crimes of mine interesting enough to win the law's attention.

But no. My crimes are sniveling and snipey, like my secret want of fellow feeling. Distain. There is no sentence to fit that crime. Unless you give the person life. That would do it.

"Who's that?" I say to Bob.

"The football coach," he says.

"I thought he was supposed to die in the plane crash."

"He was." Bob sounds put out. "But he decided to drive home, not fly."

There's always one.

"How's your coffee?"

"It's fine," I say. "I'm fine." Preemptive me.

And that's pretty much the movie. Moans and giggles from the lumberjacks, then something like a snore, Bob's periodic pat-downs of his pockets, cell phone blue light beams, football practice, human spirit sightings on the celluloid screen, punctuated by inquiries as to my well-being.

The coffee is good.

There will have been that.

But we're in the market for something more here. And so we get drunk and make out with strangers in modern movie multiplexes, people die, whole planeloads full, and we sit and fiddle with our phones and medicate ourselves with coffee beans.

"I'm sorry about the cell phone," Bob says as we each make a production of pulling on our sweaters once we're in the lobby.

"Were you expecting a call?" I say. That mean.

"There's this guy," he says. "Well I take him out for a meal on Sundays. He calls a lot to check on that. He's got early Alzheimer's. He isn't more than 50. I used to do his dad's electrical work, then the dad died. I don't really know him very well. I just take him out to eat. He calls a lot."

"That's really nice of you to take him out," I tell Bob, and it is. *But you don't answer*, I want to say to him. *You check your phone in the movie, every time he calls, but you don't answer.*

That's the thing. Somebody takes us all out to dinner. Every Sunday. Because they used to do our dad's electrical work before he died. But . . . they don't answer when we call them, I mean, not if they're in a movie. And we call and call, because we are never sure, or if we are, we can't remember just what day it is.

"Are you all right?' Bob says.

He's a nice man, he really is.

"Are you all right?" he says.

"Of course not," I say.

I'm giving him the only hopeful answer that I know.

I mean, imagine.

This, my life. I, all right.

.5 YEARS IN TOKYO DANNY MILLER

BEFORE WE LEAVE FOR JAPAN I have a nightmare. In it we move to Japan and have nowhere to live. Maybe I'm a little bit old for a nightmare. Twelve going on thirteen. We get off the plane and this metropolis, all skyscrapers and elevated highways, is full. In my dream Tokyo is this breathing, seething dread, with only artificial light. We cough up its black poison. We have to live on the streets and we don't have a phone and we can't talk to anyone. We end up sleeping in the corner of a small Japanese cafeteria where we are required to slurp when we eat our noodles. I wake up the next day and tell my mom. She hugs me, tells me not worry, that we'll find a house. I feel better.

FIVE OUT OF THE SIX OF US left from Orlando International Airport in the summer of 1998. Carly, fifteen years old, was absent, on a mission trip to England. So it was Mom, Dad, Lily, Victoria, and me. Lily was ten—she cut her hair like a boy and looked like a smaller, more popular version of me. Victoria was eight—still chubby, still content. Our friends came all the way down to the gate to wave us off on our big adventure. Before 9/11 you could do that. We each had backpacks full of snacks and magazines and Game Boys. I felt like a soldier going off to war, or an explorer off to conquer a new land. Japan, just like France before it, would fall at the feet of the Miller family. We were going to suck the marrow out of that island nation and return home in three years, stronger and more cultured. Everyone gathered around the gate and hugged and kissed and cried, said their goodbyes.

Right before we boarded our plane Carol came streaking down the concourse. Carol was my mother's close friend and her children were my close friends. She was the common-law wife of a Native American artist that worked for my father. And she sped right past my mother to Dad. She hugged him, and we were all so emotional, we explorers, that we didn't really notice too much then. But later on, it became a moment we could all point at and say—*there, that's when we should have known.*

OUR HOUSE IN TOKYO, in Denenchofu up the hill from Kohombutsu station, was big. It looked like a doctor's office. It resembled a roll of toilet paper on top of a shoebox. The exterior was coated in little tiles. A camera by the front door connected to a monitor in the kitchen so we could buzz people in. Or more frequently, force Victoria to dance in front of it for her entrance. The house had three stories, four bathrooms, five bedrooms, a sauna, a rooftop deck, and a catacomb-like basement crawlspace. It had no backyard. There wasn't space for one. Our home was squeezed into that tightly packed city of high rises and highways like a dictionary on a shelf of paperbacks. The fact that it was a house and not an apartment was almost alarming.

When we got out of the car that took us home from the airport that first day, the first thing that we did was run into the bathroom. We'd heard about the Japanese toilets. The thrones each had a side panel filled with buttons. The first button I pressed caused a probe to extend towards the center of the bowl and then a powerful stream of water shot upward, hard enough to hit the bathroom ceiling. Japan was awesome. The bidet was built in, along with a dryer like those next to sinks in public restrooms, except that it dried your butt. The toilet also had a seat warmer, for those cold Tokyo nights.

We ran around the house that first day, feeling the heated granite floors in my room and running the stairs to the roof. Examining the black wood kitchen with hidden cabinets. Laughing at the rice maker on the counter and the rice dispenser under the sink. The Japanese with their rice, tell me about it.

We settled in. We mocked the Japanese, with their miniature technology and codes of conduct. We acted Japanese, with our personalized chopsticks and our exotic meal selections. Our family made a go of it in Japan. Dad's job provided a higher standard of living than what we could afford in Orlando. What wasn't to like?

"I DON'T WANT TO LEAVE THIS FAMILY. At least I don't think that's what I want," Dad said. He was crying in the living room on the second floor of the big doctor's office looking house he dragged us across the world to live in. Victoria and Lily on the couch with Mom, her face red and blotchy, tissues in hand. Dad in the chair. The first time I ever saw my father cry. We'd only been in Japan for two months. Things weren't going so great anymore. I couldn't help but think that all these new problems, Dad and all his questions, had something to do with Carol—running through the airport to hug him goodbye. Now, years later, it's so obvious it hurts.

"I don't know how it's going to work out. I'm not saying that we are definitely going to get divorced. Maybe we just take a vacation without Mom every now and then. I would love to go to Montana," Dad said. We were all surprisingly okay with that idea. Montana sounded good. To keep them from separating I would have gone anywhere, with anyone. Dad shut the black fridge in the black wood Japanese kitchen. I stood by the rice maker.

"Yeah, Montana sounds good."

"If you go to Montana you are sure as hell taking me," Mom said. She was angry but still joking. We laughed nervously at her.

Mom ended up with custody. We ended up in Hawaii, Bali, Yellowstone, Mexico, San Diego, Hong Kong, Macau, and The Keys without her. But not Montana.

THE SECOND TIME I SAW MY FATHER CRY was when he walked into the TV room, on the other side of the house from the living room. Carly, my oldest sister, back from England, was with him. I had been watching MTV, laughing at Japanese pop acts. Dad had a scribbled note in his hand. Carly didn't cry. "We are going to look for Mom," she said.

They went out. I didn't tell Victoria or Lily what happened. That Mom left a note and was gone. Or that Carly and Dad were looking for Mom who was looking for a train. She wanted to die like the suicidal Japanese middle class, on the tracks. My mother went to the station and stared down at the metal rails. It was raining. She must have had running eye makeup and wet clothes and her broken heart on her sleeve because my mother, even in the best of times, has never been able to disguise her feelings. She stood there, looked at her future alive and her future dead—a distinctly shorter future. She thought about all of us back at the house, those that knew what she went to do and those that didn't. She went to a park and cried on a bench in the rain. A Japanese woman approached her. My mother still claims that even if maybe that woman wasn't an actual angel, God sent her. And it wasn't like that woman fixed my mother's problems. She saved her from death, and sent her back to a lot of really painful years.

"Where is your home?" my mother's Japanese angel woman said. "Go to your home." She gave my mother an umbrella.

It wasn't much of a home but my mother knew exactly where to go. Two hours after she left to kill herself and about thirty minutes after my Dad and Carly had come back without her, Mom showed up. And my Dad was crying, and I knew it was because he thought it was his fault. But he wasn't crying because she would have been gone, he was crying over his guilt, and I should have known then, too. Later his tears became one of those things that I look back on, and they make more sense. They were part of a growing list of evidence—*This one, here is where I should have known*—but I was twelve. And already Japan was becoming pretty difficult.

* * *

We didn't know anyone in Tokyo. We arrived in Japan in July but school didn't start until September. The summer was largely unoccupied. Lily, always popular, always liked, spent a few days hanging out with an old friend who lived in Tokyo, but the girl moved back to Florida two weeks after we arrived. They smoked fake cigarettes in Ginza. Carly met an ugly Japanese girl who spoke limited English and tried to be her friend. The girl's hair smelled horrible. They went to a museum and to a park, and they spent time at our house once. That relationship didn't last.

I skateboarded down the street to the train station, through the market where the shop owners shouted at me and the Japanese schoolgirls giggled and cooed. I skateboarded through the park by our house, where the old men and women did Tai Chi in the mornings. I tried to ollie onto the planters and grind the rails, with little success. An old woman, fresh from Tai Chi, rebuked me and pointed angrily at a sign that I couldn't read that apparently told me that I couldn't do what I was doing.

Carly didn't like Japan, and she always was asking me if I wanted to go home, too. I did, but I never told her that. I wanted to support Dad, besides in Florida our house wasn't near as big as this one. At home the side mirrors on our car didn't retract for tight alleys.

Sitting on the couch watching some stupid Japanese television show one day, Lily turned and asked me, "Danny, do you think Mom and Dad are going to get divorced?"

I patted her on the shoulder and responded, "Mom and Dad will never get divorced. They've been married for seventeen years." That was what I was working with. That kind of confidence. Despite all that I'd heard about Dad and Carol and all those painful family talks. Even though almost every night a family member or friend from the States called and tried to counsel Dad or Mom. Back home the troops were trying to rally for our family. But they were thousands of miles away. Useless. Despite all that, I knew my parents wouldn't divorce. When Lily asked me that question I thought of a moment years before. We had been driving in the car, home from school or to school—we were just around the corner from our house, by the graveyard.

"Mom, if Dad died, would you remarry?" I asked. She said that she would never love another man.

"If you died, would Dad remarry?' I asked. Mom said that if she was dead, she hoped Dad would remarry, because she loved him so much, she just wanted him to be happy.

Almost as soon as school started, I was on the wrong end of abuse from my classmates. Entering ninth grade I was younger than everyone else, just turning thirteen. Already, they were calling me gay and fag and telling me they were gonna kick my ass. A particular assailant would call out in the halls between classes.

"Miller. GAY!" The other kids would laugh. They'd shoot sidelong stares my way. I didn't get much relief.

I was angry at school. Those stupid little kids with parents in the Foreign Service made fun of me. Especially that stupid boy from Botswana who came to my house and played Nintendo 64 before he realized that I wasn't cool enough. I thought being on the football team would make me popular. But I wasn't any good.

Carly's first day of tenth grade ended with vomiting in the bathroom. She called in sick a few times in her two weeks there, and then she transferred to the girls' school. She hated school, the same as she hated Japan.

One day when Carly was giving Victoria a bath, Victoria noticed Carly's head twitching to the side. Turning her body around. Like a dog chasing its tail. A few days later, Mom found Carly on the floor of her bedroom, unconscious, naked. She'd had a seizure. It was supposed to be her first day at the girls' school with the uniforms.

Carly and Mom left Japan the day that would have been Carly's second day at the girls' school. After Mom and Dad had seen the counselor twice. After Dad told me that it would be easier if Mom wanted a divorce too. After Carly had a seizure and the Japanese doctors couldn't diagnose her. They couldn't fix her. Maybe the best Japanese doctors didn't speak English. Or it was just a better idea for Mom and Carly to go home and see American doctors. So my Mom kissed me goodbye, before school, the morning after Carly's seizure, and they left. We didn't see them again until Christmastime. If we were an expedition this would be where the party split up. That's never a good sign. We didn't want to do it, but this was survival. They left quickly. It was October. Carly still doesn't remember much about Japan. Or most of the next nine months. Sometimes I'm jealous.

BEFORE THE FAMILY MOVED to Tokyo, Dad was already there working and searching for a house. He applied for visas and picked furniture. He was gone for three months. Mom found out that he was calling Carol almost every day from Japan. I don't even know how she figured it out. But he was talking to her more often than he talked to Mom or us. He said they were just friends and he was telling her about Japan. Mom, fearing the worst, asked him to stop speaking with her. And Dad said no. Mom didn't know how to respond, she just thought it would all settle itself when the family moved over. Mom knew at least something about them—she caught them kissing at that party. But they were both drunk that night. And how could you continue an affair across the globe?

* * *

Mom and Carly left Japan in October. Sometime in late November Dad shaved Victoria's head. That would have never happened if Mom were with us in Japan. Mom would have patiently—like she'd done before—picked out all the lice and nits one by one while Victoria cried. I wasn't about to start picking them out. Carly would have been the second most likely to spend the time combing through her hair, but she was gone too. So nine-year-old Victoria was bald and it wasn't like we didn't get made fun of enough as it was on the bus. Victoria was chubby and short and had been taught to speak her mind, and now she looked like a boy. People made fun of my new little brother and I tried my best to defend her. But I was no hero; I had my own problems with bullies. We had fallen to the bottom rung; even the kids who were routinely teased and abused would gang up on us—happy to finally have someone to release their frustration on.

The American therapist Dad brought us to made us stand up and arrange each other like dolls, representing the way we saw the family. We were dragged to see this woman, who ran her sessions from her stuffy apartment across town. It was only Victoria, Lily, Dad, and me. In Victoria's depiction of our family everyone was having a great time but her. While we partied and showered in cash, Victoria was forgotten in her room weeping, with a shaved head (which was accurate) and no friends (also accurate). Victoria's overall depiction was not true, of course, but in therapy all feelings are honored, even those that I found ridiculous. So I couldn't shove her, or tell her she was stupid or anything like that. I still wanted to defend Dad when Victoria took his flexible body, like a giant bearded Ken doll, and put him outside the house and away from us in her arrangement.

Before we left the States our parents had thrown big parties at our house, with all the artists and designers and project managers my father worked with smoking and drinking and dancing and making fools of themselves. Eventually someone would jump into the pool with their clothes on. Us kids hid out in my bedroom, with the kids of our parents' friends, forced into a monkish state of higher morality by our parents' indecency. We complained about their drinking and played board games. That's when Mom found Dad kissing Carol, at one of those big parties. He was drunk, though. So was Carol. Mom was drinking some too. Anyways it was a party. She was one of Mom's best friends.

Lily's little room in Japan was stacked high with wrapped Christmas presents. She had carefully selected gifts for relatives and friends, most of whom she, at eleven, had never purchased for. And we couldn't figure it out. We all got the same allowance, and I blew mine on Pocari Sweat from vending machines or on video games at the arcade. For a time we all thought that she had become an impeccable money manager. One day Dad came home from work and reached into his pocket, grabbing a handful of change to drop into his can. His tired hand bumped into it, feeling its unimpressive weight. In Japan, coins reach into much higher denominations than American money and he estimated that he'd had more than three hundred dollars worth of yen in that jar. But it was near empty when he spilled it open. He found his change can's top cut off and carefully placed back on, and the can almost empty.

He immediately thought of the piles of presents that Lily had in her room, and the bragging she had openly done about her selfless purchasing. When Dad found about a hundred dollars in Lily's room she burst into tears. With bloodshot eyes and with tears she screamed and she begged to be forgiven, not only forgiven but allowed to keep buying presents. She just wanted to make everyone happy at Christmas. To fix things. Dad decided to let Lily keep the presents she had already bought.

We got off the plane in Orlando. Christmastime. My aunt and cousin had planned on coming to see us in Japan for Christmas. They were going to take the Concorde. But things changed. We disembarked, a bunch of failures. We were greeted by the same friends who had seen us off not long before. It was an inversion of our departure. This time there was no crying, no smiling. No high hopes. The only thing missing was Carol, who had since moved to California. We stumbled out of the gate like the remains of a failed expedition, frostbitten and diseased. Down one marriage.

Mom was late getting to the terminal to meet us. She had to get Carly a wheelchair. We ran into her wheeling Carly up as we passed a magazine stand in the terminal. She hugged and kissed me like she'd thought she might never see me again. She exchanged greetings with my father. I intently watched them look at each other. I searched their faces, digging for anything to give me a little bit of hope.

I rode home from the airport in my best friend's car. His family was among those there to greet us. I sat in the back of his dad's Suburban, quiet, while he tried to fill me on all the pop culture I had missed in just six months. "Flagpole Sitta" by Harvey Danger, he thought that was a really cool song. I didn't feel like I was gone long enough to care.

After an uncomfortable Christmas where Dad insisted on coming with us to Miami to celebrate the holidays with my mother's extended family, Dad left the little temporary house by the lake with the boats (ski and pontoon) and went to the airport and back to the big house in Tokyo, to go back to work. We weren't moving back there with him. He left me there in the living room with a sick sister, a thief sister, and a sister with a shaved head. He left me there with a broken mother. He touched Mom's face while she cried and then he walked out the door. I wanted to kill him. He told us he would see us soon, but it was more than six months.

* * *

A MOMENT STICKS WITH ME. Just an instance. Another puzzle piece that nestles in tight, fitting with the rest of the pieces. They tell the story of my family's fragmentation. A year before my family packs up and goes to Japan, long before we know that Dad is gonna leave, Carol drives me down the dirt road to her house in Orlando. She smokes with the windows closed, which gives me a headache. I'm too young to ask her to stop. She's taking me to her house to visit her kids, my friends.

"Do they always fight that much?"

"They fight some," I say. I don't know why she cares.

"They fight a lot," she responds, pretty quickly. She takes a drag off her cigarette and exhales in my direction. I cough. The long, bumpy road shakes the car and rattles my head.

A SHORT HISTORY OF FAILURE TOM PAUL BIRD

*"Stop trusting in man who is but a breath
in his nostrils; of what account is he?"*
—Isaiah 2:22

1.
Eve, having forgotten the facts of life,
Lost her argument with the devil,
While Adam—distracted and sulking,
Because the serpent hadn't spoken to *him*,
Chose to ignore the consequences of his pride.

He later recalled just outside
The Gates of Eden, the flaming sword
Still throwing off heat after all these years,

*Feeling my lips and tongue
Being pulled away from the inside,
Resignation settled on my silence
Like heavy dust. I could not respond—
Even as my eyes envisioned a wilderness
Stretching afar until time had no more reign
                             or desire.*

Eve, angry and frustrated at Adam's impotence,
Spent her days writing postcards to old friends:
Wish you were here; it's much lonelier than paradise.

2.
Adam continued his story—
One eye on the wrath of God,
The other on the dust,

A SHORT HISTORY OF FAILURE

Packed hard at his feet,

Back and forth we came, looking for
The familiar. Yet, somewhere along the way
The distance became too much, the maps
All neatly drawn on the back of our hands fading.
It was lengths of time like long tangled strings
That we were caught up in.
For the old places had changed;
Old voices were gone, taking with them
The old truths, the old meanings.
New voices had entered, and we no longer
Understand the language. Our favorite
Stories —the histories of our young lives,
Written out on crumbling tablets, had been
Wiped away countless times.

All the while, Eve continued to scribble
On postcards—her frustration ever growing
At the lack of response she received.

3.
While his old eyes searched
The dimming horizon for a clue,
Adam recalled a moment he
Experienced a long time ago.

I remember one evening . . .
The early spring air was exceptionally warm;
The heavens could not discern the contradiction.
Soon the confused sky rumbled; the rain came
And I knew tomorrow would be colder.
It was then I understood: Innocence is perhaps
Too heavy a memory for anyone to bear.

Eve sighed at the story and silently
Returned to her correspondence—
Hoping for just one more good day.

THE JOB POEMS SARAH GAJKOWSKI-HILL

I.
And the Lord Said to Satan, "Now put forth your hand and touch his bone and his flesh . . . He is in your power; only spare his life . . ."
　　—Job 2:6

when the gods become jealous, you might as well
drink your fill than smear ashes: the stamps will
re-echo on your skin, regardless.
i didn't think you could wring any more out of me,
what with the heat you strung into my veins
the cauterization of the seams in my hands
the dark locust wind

a rustling—unquiet; but not what i expected.
a wavering track: a voice, the uncertain steps
of a dying animal. the vaudevillian timing of it all:
when the red-clawed, crab-walk of him
began, back and forth again.
the fates have a pair of scissors
baal has a goblet of mutterings
he has a scythe
snap dragon: my bright colors pop.
i separate from the stalk.

II.
"My blackened skin falls away from me; the heat scorches my very frame . . ."
　　—Job 29-30

admittedly
this is as close to the end we've ever been—
everything is much more orange, eerily,
than I'd imagined.

THE JOB POEMS

in a dire rain of last straws
which one will stick?

this one:
it's as though you splayed my hand
indiscriminately
and loosed just one
as I slept

when you move on
unslotted and glued to the belief
that my phone dials itself

except for one deft
tug at my bow mouth,
i will merely finish out the night.

itching because you aren't there,
throbbing because you never were.

III.
Then his wife said to him, "Are you still holding to your innocence? Curse God and die."
    —Job 2:9

treason!
he calls me out
and my rage stiffens me
aghast at the tyranny of pillar smoke and
a salty sister,
no willing player
and drugged with myrrh wine
my burnt offerings will be to a vindicator
i will place my stillborn children at their altars
and of that insistent horror
i will make tiny throats
initiate a mere chord in the anthem of my screams
gag, vomit, we are all cracked clay
in this desert where
the snake's forked tail grinds

IV.
"Man born of woman is short-lived and full of trouble, like a flower that springs up and fades."
    —Job 14:1-2

you were confused with creation
as I felt our creation kick
nestled, shaded
plucked and pink

that is where your deviant history
sinister as a night-garbed mob
swept in and overtook
see it played out:
the razing of an idol,
the pillage of a daughter,
you say I am only a whisper in the face of a storm:
a pane blows with hideous cackles,
a tree uproots
and the ocean of His vengeance is out.

V.
"Oh that you would hide me in the nether world and keep me sheltered till your wrath is past!"
    —Job 14:13

the children have gone purple
and withered, little olive plants
dried gourd rattles
i lay them down amid a racket of scales, shaking
my wife dead of a thousand hemorrhages
she was white and light as a cloak, set down:
our scorched harvest
the wrinkled fruit's been barreled
the mold climbs the underside of the meat
drop the cleaver—
i need a sweet relief, release,
and something to ride out
disaster—a clean, flat land.
this table's a wasteland wide

CREATOR, AUTHOR OF THE FOOL'S CANARD RICK MULLIN

Creator, author of the fool's canard
of crossing to creation, captured where
economies of scale engage—regard
the brutal neighbors, God, your sullen heirs!

Executors of your divinity
declared an endless war. But could they find
the stone we perched upon your tomb, or see
the logic of your wrathful, errant mind?

Erase this math where two and two come four,
unwind our hearts so we might disengage
from their domain and disinherit war.
Exempt us from this Messianic age.

For, God, their vision and its spawn are one—
the neighbor's kid, his Hummer, and the gun.

IN ANOTHER UNIVERSE M. L. LIEBLER

Tomorrow the edge will appear
Far off in some distant cry that has been
Cut through wailing cliffs of horizontal
Clouds that lie like smoke
At the ends of our lives.

The clock yawns
At daybreak. Or, God's fire
Starts in the heart
To burn the soul free from sin.

Once I was
A boy before I was
Born, a simple life crawling in
A twilight circle
Where stars sleep
In the minutes of day.

I wonder if all
The anger I have ever felt
was really just the soul rubbing
Against the blue gun trigger
Of life.   Now, I wonder
If it is a lie told
As truth in another
Universe?

NOTRE DAME ALIENE PYLANT

              stones. The thrust
              f certainty in flight
              eight, a trust

              nade cruciform,
              ked the spirit's labyrinth at night
              ed form.

Words are unseen stones with which the mind
can build a temple or a crypt—a recondite
construction where belief's consigned.

In the darkest corner of this citadel
above a sea of burning stars there shines
a wooden virgin, mater-demoiselle,
an icon of obedience to words. Remorse lines
her vitreous blue eyes. She sees me too well.

TETRAGRAMMATON MARC SHAW

You've been hollowed out, O G-d.
The perfect form is no longer in you.
I cannot speak your name,
I do not even know how.
You've been set at one remove, cut crosswise
in the middle.
You've been flattened,
Straightened,
A gap between two consonants
And who knows what else lies there,
Unaccounted for.

Once incalculable,
you have become a measured thing,
a school boy's geometry problem,
hyphenated, like a run-on
sentence.

I've stepped outside your circle,
Creation's boundaries.
I slither and
twist
through the rest
of your name,
Finding foothold on the bulb of your d,
Just to slip down the other side,
dizzy and displaced,
to come out
at the bottom,
on the ledge

at the edge of knowing—
that precipice of
some other
language
entire.

AUTHOR BIOS

AN INTRODUCTION TO OUR AUTHORS

ALAN ACKMANN
SWIMMERS INTO CLEANNESS LEAPING
Fiction

Alan Ackmann graduated from the MFA fiction program at the University of Arkansas. His work has appeared in *McSweeney's*, *Louisiana Literature*, *Ontario Review*, and elsewhere. He was a Tennessee Williams scholar at the 2007 Sewanee Writers' Conference and teaches at DePaul University. Check out his website at www.alanackmann.com.

DAVID BEDSOLE
FINDING THE RING
MY THERAPIST SAYS I NEED TO LEARN GRACE
PRISON WORK
Poetry

David Bedsole has a short attention span. He likes cookbooks and modern novels. He plays the drums badly. He plays the piano fairly well, but writes all of his songs on the guitar. When he's not doing any of this, he hangs out with with his wife, Katharine, and his dog, Shiloh, teaches at a small Christian college in South Carolina, and tries to be a poet. His poems are also forthcoming in *Xavier Review*. Catch up with David at www.punkisrael.typepad.com.

CINDY BEEBE
TRANSFORMATION
Poetry

Cindy Beebe is a married mother of two who works with at-risk children and youth in inner city Memphis, near her home in Collierville, Tennessee. Her poems have been published or are forthcoming in *The Southern Review*, *Midwest Quarterly*, *Rock & Sling*, *Sow's Ear Poetry Review*, and *Grasslimb*, among others. Having written reams of poetry as a child, followed by nearly nothing for many years, she regrets her lack of formal education in creative writing (which would have been easier to manage when her parents were paying for college, as opposed to now, when she has no money).

KELLY BELMONTE
THE READING
Poetry

Consultant and strategic planner by day, Kelly Belmonte is the wife of historian Kevin and mother of 17-month-old mad scientist and lay preacher Samuel. Kelly graduated from Gordon College eons ago with a BA in English Literature and is currently pursuing a MS in Project Management from New England College so that she can sport a few more letters on her resume. She enjoys peek-a-boo, hide-and-seek, and many other games that make her son laugh. Kelly also can be found occasionally shooting hoops, swimming, gardening, reading murder mysteries, conducting writing workshops, and climbing up the slide at the playground.

TOM PAUL BIRD
A SHORT HISTORY OF FAILURE
Poetry

Tom Bird has been writing poetry off and on for thirty plus years. It's only lately that he's aspired again to see his poems in print. He's played a number of roles in life: Soldier, layabout, laborer, drafter, designer, supervisor. Currently he pastors a small church in the Adirondak Mountains of New York State.

HOLLY CARTER
PREGNANT AND UNWED ON A SMALL CHRISTIAN CAMPUS IN KIRKLAND, WASHINGTON
Poetry

Holly Carter graduated with a BA in English from Northwest University. Although she was raised in Puyallup, Washington, she currently resides in Illinois with her husband, Stephen, and their mutt, Tucker. Holly enjoys running as well as reading and writing. They hope to make their home in Omaha, Nebraska.

LINDSAY CRANDALL
A WIFE OF NOBLE CHARACTER
AN ADAM OF MY OWN
BATHSEBA AND THE KING
Poetry

Lindsay Crandall was born and raised in Rochester, New York. She received a BA in English and a BA in Communication from Roberts Wesleyan College in 2003. She married her husband, Adam, in June of 2005 and they promptly moved 1,200 miles away from home to the gulf coast of Alabama. Lindsay then worked as a IT tech temp, a newspaper editor, and a high school English teacher, all while working on her MA in English/Creative Writing from SUNY Brockport. She received her degree in 2006. Lindsay is a voracious reader and she spends a lot of time watching films, listening to music, playing with her dog, hanging with her husband, and basically wreaking havoc upon Baldwin County, Alabama.

EDMUND DE CHASCA
EPITHALAMIUM
Editor's Choice for Fiction

Edmund de Chasca's fiction has appeared in various literary journals and anthologies, including *The Green Hills Literary Lantern*, *Chautauqua Literary Journal*, *Real*, and *Under the Arch: St. Louis Stories*. A book of literary history, *John Gould Fletcher and Imagism*, was published by the University of Missouri Press. He is Senior Editor of *Boulevard* magazine.

SUZANNE RAE DESHCHIDN
SUNSET YEARS
Poetry

Suzanne Rae Deshchidn is a confessional free verse poet, freelance editor, and homeschooling mom of hispanic and native (Isleta Pueblo) heritage. She will be published in *Paterson Literary Review* Issues 36 & 37, as well as *LIPS Journal*. She was featured in *Rockland Magazine*, May 2007. Suzanne's debut poetry reading was at Bluestockings in New York City. She founded and hosts two online poetry groups, as well as a poetry roundtable at Suffern Library in New York. Her interests include belly dancing and Tai Chi. Her major poetic influences of late are: Kinnell, Lorca, Flynn, Mazziotti-Gillan, Boss, Brauer, and Hafiz.

AUTHOR BIOS

LYNN DOMINA
PRODIGAL
Poetry

Lynn Domina is the author of a collection of poetry, Corporal Works. Her more recent work has appeared in *Prairie Schooner*, *The Southern Review*, *Green Mountains Review*, *Tiferet: A Journal of Spiritual Literature*, and several other periodicals. She currently lives in the western Catskill region of New York.

NICK DUMAIS
PRELUDE
Poetry

Nick Dumais teaches English in the Washington, D.C. area and is currently working on an MEd at the University of Maryland. He has published poetry and short fiction in a few tiny magazines.

CHRISTOPHER FISHER
SCARS
Editor's Choice for Creative Nonfiction

Christopher Fisher's fiction, essays, and satire have appeared in *The Wittenburg Door*, the *Thou Shalt Not* horror anthology, *Infuze Magazine*, *The Sam Houston State Review*, and in a wonderful new literary journal called *Relief*. With his loverly wife of ten years, Christopher is currently raising four children in Texas, where he works as an editor for the Office of International Criminal Justice Press. In six short months he will receive his MFA in Creative Writing from the University of Southern Maine and may very well be calling one of you dear readers to beg for a job.

NINA FORSYTHE
THING PSALM
Poetry

Nina Forsythe currently (and, she hopes, forever) lives in Frostburg, Maryland, a fantastic little town in the mountains, after having wandered from Pittsburgh, Pennsylvania, to Wisconsin, to Kansas, to Nicaragua, and to Iowa. She has an MFA from Bennington and has had poems in many journals, including the most recent issue of *Puerto del Sol*. She was raised Lutheran, got "saved" at 15, got caught up in the charismatic movement, experienced a profound transformation through reading Dutch Calvinist philosopher Herman Dooyeweerd, became a Mennonite, and is currently attending an Episcopal Church, retaining something from every tradition she's been involved with.

SARAH GAJKOWSKI-HILL
THE JOB POEMS
Poetry

Sarah Gajkowski-Hill is a writer who was born in Waukesha, Wisconsin, but currently lives in Houston, Texas, with her husband and three young children. She works for a non-profit organization called Writers in the Schools, sharing her love of creative writing with school children in the inner city of Houston. She contributes to publications such as *Arts Houston Magazine*, *CuiZine Houston*, and the *Houston Press*, writing reviews of bands, food, and art. She published her first book of poetry entitled *Distracted and Other Poems* in 2000. Her poetry has also been published in *Scribendi*, *Rectangle*, and *Pebble Lake Review*.

AUTHOR BIOS

ROSS GALE
I FELL IN LOVE WITH A PREACHER'S WIFE
Poetry

Ross Gale is a writer from Portland, Oregon. His writing career began in second grade when his essay on Martin Luther King, Jr. was entered into a writing contest. He placed runner-up behind the brown-haired girl who sat next to him. He is not bitter about it. He is also on the five-year plan for his English degree and works as a youth minister.

JUDY LEE GREEN
THE HEALER
Poetry

Judy Lee Green is an award-winning writer and speaker whose spirit and roots reach deep into the Tennessee and North Carolina Mountains. Tennessee-bred and cornbread-fed, she developed a passion for the written word at an early age when inspired to carry a notebook by *Daily Planet* girl reporter Lois Lane. Appearing in print hundreds of times, her work has received numerous awards. She lives in Murfreesboro, Tennessee, and writes about growing up in a large family with a teenage mother, daughter of a sharecropper, who married at fourteen and birthed five little babies by the age of twenty-one.

LISA OHLEN HARRIS
TORN VEIL
Creative Nonfiction

When Lisa returned to the U.S. from Damascus, Syria, she married one of her American classmates, Todd Harris. They moved to Amman, Jordan, where Todd pastored an English-speaking church and Lisa had lots of babies (actually only two of her children were born in the Middle East, if she kept a correct count. The years blur, she says). Watch for more of Lisa's creative nonfiction about living in the Middle East in Fall 2007 issues of *River Teeth* and *Arts & Letters*.

C. A. HASSELBALCH
AN ITALIAN RESTAURANT IN DOMINION
Editor's Choice for Poetry

Carol Ann Hasselbalch lives in a small southeast Texas town with her husband and four boys. She likes to read, travel, and write in that order. She graduated from Lamar University in August 2007.

MARGOT STARBUCK HAUSMANN
RELINQUISHED
Creative Nonfiction

Margot Starbuck Hausmann, a writer and speaker, lives with her husband, Peter, and children Zoe, Rollie, and Abhishek in Durham, North Carolina. A graduate of Westmont College and Princeton Theological Seminary, Margot has also served the Church as wordbearer in her work as chaplain, pastor, graphic artist, and mommy. Recent publications include *Today's Christian Woman*, *Adoption Today*, and *Rev!* Connect with Margot at www.MargotStarbuckHausmann.com.

ELLEN HERBERT
STONING, SOUTHERN BAPTIST STYLE
Creative Nonfiction

Ellen Herbert's essays have been published in *The Sonora Review*, *The Rambler*, *Alimentum*, and others. She won the 2006 Flint Hills Review Creative Nonfiction Prize and was published in it subsequently. Her latest essay was published 6/11/07 in *The Washington Post*'s "Style," which thrilled her family of origin. Her real love is fiction; it is what she buys and reads. Her novel-in-progress won a 2006 National Pen Women Award, but she has no idea whether it will be published, because agents say no one is buying or reading fiction any more. No one but her, she tells them.

SORINA HIGGINS
DAPHNE'S COMPLAINT TO SYRINX
SEMELE'S EXAMPLE
WEDDING DAY
Poetry

Sorina Higgins and her husband live in Allentown, Pennsylvania, where she teaches courses in language arts, writing, music, philosophy, Shakespeare, and *The Inklings*. Her poetry and other writings have appeared in *Innisfree*, *Studio*, *Perspectives*, *Alive Now*, *Windhover*, *Bible & Spade*, and *Idiom*. She is the author of the entry on Charles Williams in the forthcoming *Encyclopedia of Christian Literature*. A paper entitled "Heraldry of Heaven: The Development of Lewis's Sehnsucht in his Correspondence and Cultural Context" has been selected for presentation at a conference on C. S. Lewis in October.

S. R. KOVACOVIC
WINDOW WASHER
Poetry

S. R. Kovacovic lives just outside of Philadelphia. His writing career was derailed by addiction about ten years ago until around a year ago when he sobered up. In early 2007, he began writing again as a form of therapy. The result has been a load of poems, several short stories, and one manuscript for a novel. S. R. has two beautiful children with one on the way. His wife is his backbone as he was born without one, much like a salamander . . . or a worm. Yeah, a worm. Visit his website at www.myspace.com/srkovacovic.

JOSEPH LAIZURE
THE RIDER AHEAD
Fiction

Joseph Laizure is writing a novel and riding his bike in Minneapolis. His fiction has also appeared in *Third Coast*.

M. L. LIEBLER
IN ANOTHER UNIVERSE
Poetry

M. L. Liebler is the author of several books of poetry including the forthcoming book *Wide Awake in Someone Else's Dream* (Wayne State University Press 2008) and the 2001 Finalist for The Paterson Poetry Prize and winner of The 2001 Wayne State University Board of Governors' Award, *Written In Rain: New & Selected* (2000). Much of his work has been published in both national and international journals and reviews, and he has recorded CDs of poetry and music with his own Magic Poetry Band. He has taught English, Creative Writing, World Literature, American Studies, and Labor Studies at Wayne State University in Detroit since 1980.

AUTHOR BIOS

D. S. MARTIN
THE ATLANTIC
Poetry

D. S. Martin is a Canadian whose poetry has appeared in many significant journals such as *Canadian Literature*, *The Christian Century*, *Christianity & Literature*, and *Rock & Sling*. Visit his website, www.dsmartin.ca, where you'll be able to purchase his chapbook *So The Moon Would Not Be Swallowed* (Rubicon) which was published in 2007. He writes about poetry for various publications including *Books & Culture* and *Image*. He is Music Critic for *Christian Week*.

DANNY MILLER
.5 YEARS IN TOKYO
Creative Nonfiction

Danny Miller is a twenty-two year old go-getter from Orlando, Florida. He recently graduated from the University of Central Florida with a degree in Creative Writing. When he isn't writing sob stories about his upbringing, he is usually working on short films or video productions in some capacity with Rocksteady Pictures, which he founded. Danny is 65 pages through his first screenplay (written in collaboration) and in the early stages of a series of stories about a fighting rooster named The Great Satan. In November he'll marry his childhood crush and the love of his life (actually the same person!).

LINDA MCCULLOUGH MOORE
HUNDRED DOLLAR BILLS
IS ANYONE ALL RIGHT?
Fiction

Linda McCullough Moore is the author of *The Distance Between* (Soho Press). A second literary novel and a collection of short stories are currently in search of brilliant representation and/or prompt pretigious publication. Linda's award-winning short fiction appears in more than two hundred places such as *The Sun*, *The Massachusettes Review*, *Glimmer Train*, *The Southern Review*, *Queen's Quarterly*, *The Boston Globe*, and *The Alaska Quarterly Review*.

RICK MULLIN
CREATOR, AUTHOR OF THE FOOL'S CANARD
Poetry

Rick Mullin is a painter, poet, and journalist living in northern New Jersey. His paintings can best be described as representational expressionist. His poetry is almost exclusively formal, metrical verse with a heavy emphasis on the sonnet. Much of Rick's poetry deals with family issues and he writes extensively about his home state and the New York metropolitan area. He has also written light verse and travel pieces. He is currently working on a series of poems with the working title of *Stations of the Parkway*. Visit Rick online at www.cassowary.wordpress.com.

JEFF NEWBERRY
TERMINAL
A BODY'S LAMENT
SUNLIGHT SHATTERED
Poetry

Jeff Newberry is a student in the Creative Writing Program at the University of Georgia in Athens and an Assistant Professor of English at Abraham Baldwin College in Tifton, Georgia.

His poems and essays have appeared in a variety of publications, including *Copper Nickel*, *Poetry Southeast*, *The Eleventh Muse*, and *Gulf Stream Magazine*. He and his wife, Heather, welcomed their first son, Benjamin Lang, in April of 2007. The now-ousted former baby of the family, Scout the dog, is convalescing in the back yard. Find him at http://museoffireblog.blogspot.com.

DEVIN O'DONNELL
A REED SHAKEN IN THE WILDERNESS
Fiction

Devin O'Donnell lives in Santa Cruz, California with his wife and two children. He teaches English at a college preparatory school. He holds a BA in Journalism and is studying for a master's degree in humanities and literature. He writes because he must, but tries not to make an idol of it. He was recently published in *The Ankeny Briefcase*, an anthology of short fiction from the Burnside Writers Collective.

ALIENE PYLANT
NOTRE DAME
Poetry

Aliene Pylant serves as an adjunct faculty member at Richland College in Dallas, Texas, where she teaches creative writing in a program designed for survivors of traumatic brain injury. Every semester her students teach her the meaning of courage and perseverance.

JENNA RISANO
WHAT WOULD JESUS WEAR?
Poetry

Jenna Risano is just your everyday liberal Catholic poet. She is a junior at the University of Tampa, double majoring in Writing and English. She would like to thank her family for their love, the UT English/writing department for their support, and Sister Pat for scaring the crap out her.

MARC SHAW
TETRAGRAMMATON
Poetry

Hailing from Frankfurt, Germany, Marc Shaw is a recent graduate of the Theology and the Arts program at Fuller Theological Seminary with an emphasis in Literature and Poetry. He currently teaches high school English in Los Angeles. He enjoys jumping up and down at random intervals, singing in the shower, and throwing things at his students. He also enjoys Billy Collins, William Blake, Wendell Berry, Van Morrison, and Bob Dylan. He is currently applying to various PhD programs in English Literature around the country. Visit Mark online at mshaw50g.blogspot.com.

TRISTA SWING
KNOWING TOO MUCH
PARENTS
Poetry

Trista Swing lives in a tiny one-bedroom apartment with her newlywed husband in Boston, Massachusetts. During the day she works as a marketing coordinator for a textbook publisher. At night she enjoys walking around the city with her husband, or playing with their new pet, the robot vacuum. Trista received her master's degree in creative writing from Texas Tech

University. She was a semi-finalist for the 2005 "Discovery"/ The Nation Prize, and her poems have appeared in *The Minnesota Review*, *32 Poems*, and *Albatross*.

J. MARCUS WEEKLEY
LITTLE GIRLS
Poetry

J. Marcus Weekley was born in Chattanooga, Tennessee. His writing appears in *from four years*, *Look Out Below and Other Tales*, and other books (www.lulu.com/whynottryitagain), as well as the journals *Quick Fiction*, *Versal*, *Poetry International*, and others. Marcus became a believer a while ago but is still learning what it means to walk with God. Marcus is also a photographer, and his images accompany the essays of Gail Folkins in *Texas Dance Halls* (Texas Tech University Press, September 2007).

many voices. a single purpose.
the master's artist

what is a master's artist?

The king gestures toward the tower window, indicating a vast kingdom spreading as far as the eye can see, and says, "Son, one day all of this will be yours."

The whiny, pathetic prince glances toward the window and says, "What? The curtains?"

Thus opens one of my favorite scenes from Monty Python and the Holy Grail. "Okay," you say. "That's dandy dialog for an absurd comedy. But why use it to open a post exploring what a Master's artist is?"

I'm so glad you asked.

a master's artist is...

small...

I love the final scene of Men in Black. The camera pans up from the street, out to the city, the nation, the world, the galaxy, to infinity and beyond, and the whole ball o' wax is contained in a single marble. What a great picture of how tiny we are! Of course, the good news is we're not being tossed around by aliens in some cosmic game. We're held in the palm of Almighty God, who transcends time and space and all created things. He can swirl galaxies in a celestial hoedown and still catch every silent tear shed in secret.

an heir...

Sometimes I think we're a lot like that wimpy prince. Our Father has given us great and glorious promises regarding our inheritance, but we can't see past the curtains. We set our hopes on things that are passing away—contracts, reputation, success, money—when God is gesturing at eternity and saying, "I have so much more for you."

a mirror...

Whether we like it or not, we are God's image to the world, and we have an obligation to keep ourselves unstained. Until we get sick of our narcissism, we won't be of much use to God. A mirror has no self-consciousness. It reflects whatever it faces. A Master's artist forsakes other loves (including fascination with her own gifts), and follows hard after God. She sets her face on Jesus.

We are artists because our Father is an artist. Creativity is our birthright. In and of ourselves we are no greater than the scum under God's fingernails, but He has humbled Himself and set His love upon us. And, as if that weren't enough, He's ushered us into a broad place, tossed us the car keys, and said, "Go have fun, my obedient children. Find Me everywhere—even in Monty Python or Men in Black. Create something beautiful. Just remember, whatever you do is a reflection on Me."

Our King gestures toward the window and says, "All of this will someday be yours." Marvel, my fellow artists. He shares His inheritance with us, and we don't even deserve the curtains. —*Jeanne Damoff*

www.themastersartist.com

Christian Writing ... Unbound!

(Thank God)

Get **Relief** 4 times a year when you subscribe at www.reliefjournal.com. You save $19.76 when you subscribe, because Coach is so crazy, he's going to pay your shipping and handling for you and knock 95 cents off the cover price of each issue! Isn't that neat? We never know what he's going to do next, that crazy Coach.

So why wait? You've just read this issue and you know you liked it. Come on, now, don't lie. We know you did.
So point that web browser right over to
www.reliefjournal.com/store and subscribe today!

COACH'S MIDNIGHT DINER IS NOW AVAILABLE AT THE RELIEF STORE!

GO TO A COMIC BOOK CONVENTION WITH JESUS AND CHRIS MIKESELL

VISIT THE NEXUS OF THE UNIVERSE WITH KEVIN LUCIA

EVANGELIZE AT GUNPOINT WITH CHARLES BROWNING

GET INTO A STREET FIGHT WITH MATT MIKALATOS

BLOW UP SOME ASTEROIDS WITH JENS RUSHING

TAKE SWIMMING LESSONS WITH NATHAN KNAPP

GET DE-MUSED WITH MIKE DURAN

DRINK A LITTLE ABSINTHE WITH MELODY GRAVES

GO TO A STRIP CLUB WITH R. M. OLIVER

HAVE A CHAT WITH ELVIS AND JENNIFER J. EDWARDS

FIND A LITTLE HELP WITH LINDA GILMORE

BUY A WHOREHOUSE WITH ROBERT GARBACZ

TAKE A TRIP TO THE MOON WITH NEIL A. RIEBE

CATCH THE NIGHT TRAIN WITH SUZAN ROBERTSON

GIVE A GIFT TO GET A GIFT WITH PAUL LUIKART

LOOK INTO THE EYES OF A GARGOYLE WITH J. MARK BERTRAND

TAKE THE CASE WITH S. J. KESSEL

FIND THE WORM IN THE APPLE WITH ROB JENNINGS

BECOME A HERO WITH MIKE DELLOSO

GO OLD TESTAMENT ON SOME BAD GUYS WITH MIKE MEDINA

TAKE A NEW LOOK AT STATUTORY VIOLENCE WITH CAROLINE MISNER

GET YOURS AT HTTP://WWW.RELIEFJOURNAL.COM/STORE!

The following bonus story is one of 21 that make up *Coach's Midnight Diner*, a genre anthology of horror, mystery, crime, and paranormal fiction. I sneak one in at the end of every issue of *Relief*. "Sanctuary" is a wonderful tale that sums up the unique reality that surrounds diners everywhere.

-Coach Culbertson, Proprietor

SANCTUARY

LINDA GILMORE

My favorite diner is a funny kind of place. Not funny like one of those pizza places where kids want you to take them, where a giant mouse greets you (which always struck me as strangely disturbing) and the kids can play games. No, it's in a seedy neighborhood and the street signs are gone—and sometimes I can't seem to find it at all. Weird. Maybe I'm just getting old. That's what my pal Harry says. He says 30 years on the night copy desk will do that to you.

One night we got off late. The shift had been a nightmare with breaking news, right on deadline no less, about shootings and scandal. The big story was an outbreak of violence between rival crime organizations. I edited most of the front section, and by the time the paper was on the press it was almost one in the morning. I was beat. One more misplaced comma or weak verb and I would have resorted to violence.

"Let's go somewhere," I said to Harry as we walked out to my car. I was too keyed up to go straight home, and besides, I didn't have anything to go home to.

"If you're going to drive around half the night looking for that diner, count me out," he said.

"Oh, come on. You know you're hungry. If I can't find it right away, I'll take you home. OK?"

"No thanks," said Harry, "I'll be sleepin' on the couch if I don't get home soon." He got in his car without looking back.

I still needed to unwind, though. I could picture the neighborhood with the diner and anticipated its warmth and light on a cold dark night. I didn't need the street signs to find it—this night I drove straight to it and parked across the street.

It seemed colder when I got out of the car. The wind swirled dead leaves and trash in eddies along the street. The city lights made the low clouds above glow softly; it felt like snow.

In the large front window a neon sign spelled out the words "Diner Open All Night." I don't know if it had another name. I'd only ever heard people call it the Diner.

Inside it was warm and fairly busy for that time of night. A couple of men sat at the counter, about a dozen others sat in booths lined along the opposite wall. It was a typical night crowd: two cops, a cab driver, four nurses in colorful scrubs, a few other people whose occupations I couldn't identify.

I sat on a stool at the counter and Mike, the cook, came to take my order. He remembered me.

"Hi Ned," he said, bringing me a steaming mug. "You look like a man who could use some coffee. Anything else?"

I ordered eggs and sausage and Mike turned to the grill. He chatted as he cooked, asking about the news. Mike's a husky guy and always pleasant, but for some reason he has the most forgettable face. When you don't see him right in front of you, you can't quite recall what he looks like. But he always remembers his customers. I hadn't been in the place for months, but he knew me right away.

Pretty soon Mike set my plate in front of me and refilled my cup. I dug straight in. Mike was some amazing cook. I don't know what he did to the food, but it seemed somehow more filling, more satisfying, than meals anywhere else. Maybe it's crazy of me to talk like this, but I don't know how else to describe it. What was on my plate looked like eggs and sausages, but it was ambrosia for the gods.

The sound of tires squealing, a door slamming, and a woman shrieking interrupted my meal. As I looked toward the entrance a young woman carrying a small boy burst in. She looked around wildly and started for the back. Mike caught up to her quickly.

"Slow down! What's wrong, ma'am?"

"Please," she said, her eyes and voice pleading, "Is there a back way out? I have to get away. He's coming!"

Mike stayed calm. "Don't worry, you'll be safe here."

Even as she shook her head and tried to pull away, we heard shouting outside.

"Becky! I know you're hiding somewhere around here. Get out here now or it'll be worse when I find you!"

A man was standing outside the diner and shouting. I expected him to come charging through the door after Becky, and it was plain from her face that she expected the same thing. But he didn't. He stood on the sidewalk, facing the diner, but his eyes scanned back and forth across the front of the building like the Diner Open All Night sign was a centerfold he couldn't get enough of. He paced back and forth, looked up and down the street, then shouted some more, but he didn't come in.

Becky was frozen where she stood, staring at the man outside who obviously couldn't see her, though the wide aisle between the counter stools and the tables was in plain view through the windows. She looked a question at Mike.

It didn't make sense to me either; but the thought came that the man couldn't see the diner right in front of his face. What other explanation could there be?

Mike just smiled at Becky.

"Like I said," he told her, "you'll be safe here. There's someone here who can help you, I think."

He guided Becky to a booth where two women were sitting and, like the rest of us, watching the drama unfold. Becky and her little boy sat and whatever the women said seemed to calm her. Mike brought her a cup of coffee and some chocolate milk for the boy.

When he came back behind the counter I asked him who the women in the booth were.

"Oh, they work at an emergency shelter. They'll know what to do."

"Huh. Two women from an emergency shelter in here, just when . . ."

Mike didn't say anything, just smiled and shrugged. I went back to eating. The food was still good, even cold.

Something in the window caught my attention, though. A boy, in a thin jacket, was watching through the window, hungry eyes following my fork's progress from my plate to my mouth. He couldn't have been more than fifteen, slight, with that gangly look that boys have about that age. What was a kid like that doing out alone in this part of town in the middle of the night? A couple possibilities I didn't want to think about came to mind.

I motioned for him to come in and he moved toward the door, then hesitated. I smiled in what I hoped was a reassuring way and motioned to him again. This time he came in, but stopped short of the counter.

"Can I buy you some breakfast?" I said.

Hunger and pride waged a war across his face. Pride won.

"I got some money." He cleared his throat to get Mike's attention. "Excuse me, mister, what can I get for a buck?"

He looked to me like he needed more than a dollar's worth of food.

"You're in luck," Mike said, with a smile. "Tonight's special is a plate of eggs, bacon and hash browns for $1."

The boy started to grin, then a suspicious look took over.

"I'm not dumb," he said. "What's the catch?"

"No catch," Mike said. "This time of night I need to use up what I've got before the morning deliveries."

The boy thought about it, looking back outside, where fat snowflakes were now drifting past the front window. I thought about how if I'd had bacon instead of sausage, I could've had hash browns, too, and saved three-fifty.

"OK," he said. "I'll have the special."

"Smart choice," I said. "Mike's a great cook. You'll see."

The boy sat down a couple of stools away. Mike brought him a cup of hot chocolate.

The boy wrapped his red hands around the cup and started to sip; his ears and nose were red with cold, and his light brown hair hung lank across his forehead. Up close I thought he looked closer to thirteen than fifteen. He reminded me of someone I used to know and for a moment I couldn't look at him. Then I pushed the memories down and said, "Son, what are you doing wandering around this time of night?"

"None of your business," he said. "Sir."

Somebody had taught the kid manners. I glanced across the diner and saw one of the cops looking our way. I didn't think the boy had noticed him, or he probably wouldn't have come in.

"Don't you think it should be somebody's business?" I asked. "Like maybe your parents?"

"No," he said. "They're the last people whose business it should be."

Mike set his plate in front of him and he started to eat, then stopped.

"I'm fine," he said. "I just got lost, that's all."

But he didn't look me in the eye.

"What's your name?" I asked.

"Da—Josh," he said, around a mouthful of eggs. He was eating like he hadn't had a good meal in a long time.

"Hi, Josh," came a voice from the other side of the boy. It was the cop who had been watching him. His nametag said his name was Brown.

Josh looked scared and started to get up, but the officer put his hand on his shoulder.

"Go ahead and finish eating," he said. "Then my partner and I would like to help you out."

"I won't go to no juvie," Josh said, a defiant edge to his voice.

"Who said anything about juvenile hall?" Officer Brown asked. "There's someone at the precinct who can make sure you end up in a safe place. Am I right that you need a safe place?"

Josh seemed to respond to the kindness in Brown's voice. He softened a little, and nodded a bit hesitantly.

"OK," Brown said. "Tell you what, I'll make Sam sit in the back and you can ride up front with me." He sat beside Josh while he finished eating and they talked quietly. I didn't catch everything they said, but it sounded like Josh had run away from a pretty bad home situation and there were younger siblings who needed help, too.

I wondered about this second coincidence, but Mike was busy behind the counter and I didn't say anything.

The diner started to empty. The cops left with Josh at the same time that Becky and her son left with the women from the shelter. Soon I was the only one left. I was reluctant to leave but it was snowing heavily and I knew it would only get worse the longer I waited. I got out my wallet to pay for my breakfast, but stopped when the front door banged open and shut behind me.

Two men stood just inside the door, snow dusting their hair and shoulders. Their dark overcoats weren't bulky enough to fully mask the shoulder holsters. I wished the cops hadn't left already. I recognized one of the men from the mug shot I'd used on the front page that very night. Sammy Sorrento, one of the lieutenants of the city's largest organized crime family.

He and his companion looked around the empty diner. They seemed a little surprised to be there, and a little afraid.

"Hey, you," Sorrento said to Mike. "What kind of joint is this?"

"It's a diner," Mike said, a bit amused, it seemed to me.

"Got a back room?"

"No."

Sorrento glanced around and grabbed his companion's arm.

"Come on Joey, let's go," he said.

"Don't worry," Mike said, coming around from behind the counter. "You'll be safe here."

Sorrento stopped, looking even more puzzled.

"No one can find you here." Mike's voice was steady and reassuring.

"What are you talking about?"

"Just what I said. Someone you don't want to find you is looking for you and you need a safe place. This is a safe place."

This was too much for me.

"Mike, what are you doing?" I said. "Don't you know who this is? You don't want to protect him from the police!"

"He's not hiding from the police," Mike said, still looking at Sorrento.

The crack and stutter of automatic weapon fire sent Sorrento and Joey diving for the floor. I ducked behind the counter. But Mike just stood in front of the door and windows as two cars came careering around the corner, guns still firing. I could see the sparks of fire from the muzzles and heard the ping of bullets hitting the building and trash cans. I expected the plate glass window to disintegrate in the barrage of bullets, but nothing touched it. Once again, the pursuers didn't seem to see the diner.

After the cars had passed, Mike stepped over the two men on the floor and looked out the window.

"I'm afraid your car is done for," he said.

Sorrento slowly got up from the floor, staring at Mike, his mouth open.

"What, what happened? I don't get this. What is this place? Who are you?" he asked.

Mike smiled again. "I told you. This is a diner. My name is Mike. Some people call me Michael."

Was it my imagination or did light flicker around Mike's head when he said that?

Fear and wonder mingled in Sorrento's expression. He crossed himself and fell to his knees. I thought I heard him muttering a Hail Mary.

"Don't be ridiculous," Mike said, embarrassed. "Get up. You need someplace safe. Help is coming, but you'll have to wait a while. Want something to eat?"

Sorrento and Joey just nodded. I could understand. I was pretty speechless myself.

Mike filled our coffee cups, then turned the heat up under the grill and began cooking more eggs and bacon. Maybe it was just the reassurance of the very ordinary act of cooking breakfast, but the aroma brought a calm to the room.

Soon Mike set plates of food in front of Sorrento and Joey.

"Weren't you going to call someone?" Sorrento asked.

"Oh, he's coming. He's a regular." Mike glanced up at the clock. "Should be here any minute."

Sorrento looked skeptically out at the snowstorm. I highly doubted that anyone else was going to come into the diner that night; you'd think I would have known better. Before long another man entered the diner, stamping his feet and brushing the snow off his coat. The stocky black man hung his coat on the coat tree by the front door and when he turned to the counter I could see his clerical collar.

Mike greeted him with a smile.

"Hi Father Jones. Quite a night, isn't it? Coffee?"

"That would be wonderful," he said, then he looked at me. "Hi. Anything I can do to help?"

I almost said yes, but just shook my head.

Father Jones turned to Sorrento, who now seemed more angry than confused.

"You said help was coming!" he yelled at Mike. "I thought you meant the FBI!"

Father Jones answered, instead.

"Of course, you'll probably need to talk to the FBI at some point, but I think you might need my kind of help first. Am I right?"

Understanding dawned on Sorrento's face.

"Yeah, I think you are."

As I got up to leave, Sorrento asked Father Jones to hear his confession. I started for the door and Mike followed.

"Goodnight, Ned," he said. "Be careful."

I suddenly remembered my car was across the street and looked out quickly to see how badly it was shot up.

"It's OK," Mike said. "Drive safe."

"I've been here before, but never seen stuff like this," I said. "What kind of diner is this, really?"

"Well, some nights are more interesting than others," Mike said. "What kind of diner do you think this is?"

I thought about it a minute.

"I think," I said, "that this is a diner that's here when I need it. God knows I needed it tonight."

"Yes, he does," Mike said. "But maybe you needed it for another reason."

"Yeah," I said. Josh's thin frame and lonely eyes came to mind. "Yeah, I think I did."

I left. As I drove home, I reflected on a man whose face I couldn't quite picture and a diner that was always there for people who really needed it. And on a boy who reminded me of the son I once had and would never see again. I'm not a man who believes in second chances much, but I suspect Mike is.

If you ever visit my city and find yourself wandering around a seedy neighborhood late at night, you might come across a diner with a neon sign that says "Diner Open All Night." And in that diner you'll find a man named Mike, or maybe it's Michael, and you most likely will find help, or will find you have help to offer. But maybe those are one and the same thing.

COACH'S MIDNIGHT DINER SPOTLIGHT AUTHOR
LINDA GILMORE
"SANCTUARY"

If Linda Gilmore were a character in the diner in her story, she'd be sitting in the back booth, drinking coffee and reading a book until the place closed. But since she's not, she works in an office and drinks coffee. She also reads lots of books, writes stories, and plays her current favorite game—Guitar Heroes II—with her teenage sons. She's been married for 29 years and lives in Kansas, which is a lot more interesting than most people think. And it's not flat.